GW01017710

RECORD (

How to find them

NINTH (2002) EDITION

Jeremy Gibson and Pamela Peskett

Federation of Family History Societies

First published by the **Federation of Family History Societies.**

Ninth edition published 2002 by
Federation of Family History Societies (Publications) Ltd.,
Units 15-16 Chesham Industrial Estate, Oram St., Bury, Lancs. BL9 6EN, England;
On-line Bookshop: www.familyhistorybooks.co.uk
Latest news and Catalogue: http://www.sales@ffhs.org.uk

First edition, 1981
Second edition, 1982, reprinted 1983
Third edition, 1985, reprinted 1986
Fourth edition, 1987, reprinted 1988
Fifth edition, 1991
Sixth edition, 1993
Seventh edition, 1996
Eighth edition, 1998
Ninth edition, 2002

Ninth edition, Copyright © Jeremy Gibson and Pamela Peskett, 2002

ISBN 1 86006 126 5

Maps devised and drawn by Pamela Peskett
Computer typesetting in Arial and layout by Jeremy Gibson

Cover illustration: The Public Record Office, Kew, specially prepared by Whitney J. Lumas III.

Printed by Parchment (Oxford) Limited

Preface

Our gratitude as always goes to all those archivists who supplied maps issued by their individual offices or specially prepared for us, answered our enquiries and supplied updated information. We are grateful too to readers who told us of amendments necessary.

In this ninth edition the outstandingly important relocations in Central London of all original records at the Public Record Office to Kew; of General Registry Office records of births, marriages and deaths to the Family Records Centre, with the G.R.O. indexes, and microfilm of census records etc. and of P.C.C. wills; and the search room and indexes of the Principal Registry of the Family Division, to all post-1857 probate records in England and Wales, to First Avenue House on High Holborn, are now familiar to most researchers. The Archive Section of Sutton Heritage Services, in south-west London, is included for the first time, and Lambeth Archives Department at the Minet Library has been reinstated.

Outside London, relocated offices have required revised or new maps of Beverley, Birkenhead, Chelmsford, Dover/Whitfield, Oxford/Cowley, Reading and Worcester. Other minor alterations have been made on advice from archivists and users. We welcome such comment and rely on constructive criticism. In addition to Email, websites are included for the first time: a marathon telephone session in mid-March 2002 means that these were up-to-date as of then. Otherwise there are the usual alterations to road systems and car-parking facilities.

The most recent changes in local government have made it difficult to equate these areas with pre-1974 counties. As most people are likely to be searching for pre-1974 ancestors, the town plans have been rearranged according to the counties as they existed at 1974 (thus Avon, Cleveland, Cumbria, Humberside, Greater Manchester, Merseyside, Tyne and Wear *et al.* and the post-1974 Welsh counties, except for Powys, disappear; whilst Dudley appears under Staffordshire, not Worcestershire).

Federation of Family History Soceties Publications Ltd. is a wholly owned subsidiary of the Federation of Family History Societies, Registered Charity No. 1038721.

CONTENTS

3

CODE OF PRACTICE FOR FAMILY HISTORIANS
USING COUNTY RECORD OFFICES

Preparation

You will find a visit to a record office much more rewarding if you do your homework beforehand and arrive well prepared. If you are a beginner your first step, before a visit, should be to read a book on how to trace your family. Excellent value for money is *Beginning Your Family History* by George Pelling, published by the Federation of Family History Societies. It is also a good idea to join a Family History Society and/or local history class in genealogy, details of which may be obtained from your Local Education Authority or Workers Educational Association. A list of the world-wide family history societies and a leaflet detailing the services of the Federation of Family History Societies and its publications can be obtained in exchange for a self-addressed, stamped envelope (or three International Reply Coupons) from the **Administrator, Maggie Loughran, FFHS, PO Box 2425, Coventry CV5 6YX**.

Contact the record office you need to use to make sure that they have the records you need to begin your research, and to discover details of opening hours etc. and whether you need to book a seat or microfilm reader. Most record offices now have basic information of this nature on a website on the Internet. They also are likely to operate a reader's ticket system, similiar to the ones in use in the Public Record Office and British Library, and many of them use the County Archive Research Network (CARN) whereby a ticket issued in one participating office is valid in others. Whatever system is operated official proof of identity, bearing name and current address, will be required before a ticket is issued. In two counties, Devon and Gloucestershire, record offices charge for access. This Guide gives addresses, telephone and fax numbers, Email and websites, and maps of location for many of the record offices in England, Wales and Scotland. Another useful guide is *Record Repositories in Great Britain*, now in its eleventh edition, published by the Public Record Office in collaboration with the Historic Manuscripts Commission. Many offices issue an introductory leaflet, and sell modestly-priced brief guides and lists of registers.

You should be quite clear about what you want to find out at the record office. This means collecting all the known facts about your family first and deciding what you hope to find out on your visit. A request for advice on ways of tracing the baptism of Mary Smith whom you believe to have been born at Spennynoor about 1825 can be answered by the search room staff quite easily. However, a long story about your family will confuse the search room staff and possibly yourself, until the point of the enquiry is lost and time wasted.

Remember to bring copies of your notes with you in case you need to refer to them and come supplied with pencils, paper (and reading glasses if you need them).

At the record office

Almost all record offices have a signing-in book which you will be expected to sign on each visit. This usually implies acceptance of the record office rules which you should read carefully on your first visit. All offices forbid smoking, eating and drinking in the search room area and this should be taken to include sweets. Many offices require you to leave outdoor clothes, bags, briefcases and large files in a reception area or locker.

Wherever possible, avoid bringing extra people with you. Most offices have no room for people not engaged in research. Some offices may allow you to bring in a baby or a young child provided there is no disturbance to other readers but you should always check on local practice before making a visit. If disturbance is caused, you should leave the office yourself rather than waiting to be asked to do so. You will not be allowed to bring animals into a record office.

When you arrive, a member of staff will explain how to use the indexes and catalogues, or point you to relevant leaflets or instruction notices. You will also be shown how to order the records you wish to use, usually by filling in an application form. If you find a reference in an index, it is always best to check the catalogue entry for further information before ordering the document. If you don't find the information you require in the first place you look, other sources can probably be suggested.

Speak as quietly and as little as possible. If you have come with other people, divide the work up as well as you can and leave the search room if you need to discuss it. Nothing is more annoying to other readers than a running commentary between two readers on the progress of their work.

The use of tape recorders, typewriters, laptop computers and cameras, if permitted in a record office, must be established beforehand and prior permission obtained.

Make sure that you have returned your records and packed up before the stated closing time, so that you can leave promptly at that time.

Using the records

When original records are produced for you, remember that they are unique sources of information, which must survive to serve future generations as well as our own. Treat them with great care. Most record offices require the use of pencil only, and sometimes expect you to wear thin cotton gloves (provided by the office). Do not run a pencil or your finger down the record, or rest your paper on it while writing. Staff will always provide advice on how to handle documents safely.

It will be to your advanatge directly, and to the archivists' ultimately, to make notes as carefully and specifically as possible. Always head them with the proper reference to the document from which the information comes, and describe exactly the extent of the search made, *e.g.* "searched 1700-1720 and all Smith entries noted" or "failed to find marriage of John Smith 1700-1720, though there are other Smith marriages, not noted". If you are methodical, it will save you having to re-use the records unnecessarily.

If you work backwards in your family history, which is always advisable, you should find that you can read the more difficult earlier forms of handwriting without too much trouble. Archivists will generally help with a few difficult words, but have no time to sit down and read extensive passages. They can recommend books which will help you in this field.

As you develop your history, you may extend your searches into documents which need more skill to understand, such as deeds and manorial records. Again archivists can in some instances assist and suggest helpful books.

When documents are finished with, the utmost care should be taken in returning them exactly as they were received. In strong rooms where millions of documents are stored, misplaced documents are virtually impossible to trace except by chance, so one wrongly folded inside another may be 'lost' for years. Find out from the staff where documents which you have finished using should be returned. Some offices will require you to hand them to a member of staff and wait while they are checked, and in many cases the number of items produced at one time will be limited.

Owing to problems of wear and tear from excessive use, more and more records are being produced to searchers in the form of microfilm or fiche. Microfilm copies held elsewhere, such as the census returns, may also be available. These too must be treated with care. Most offices require roll film to be wound back to the spool it was on to begin with. This is particularly important where the office operates a self-service system for microfilms.

Postal and telephone enquiries

If you are unable to visit a record office, it may still be possible for you to obtain the information you need. Though an extensive search is usually better carried out personally, some offices will carry out a minor search involving a small number of years in a single parish, without charge. Others will make a charge, and others again will only answer enquiries as to records held and will not search within them. Most offices will be able to supply you with a list of record searchers who will carry out searches for you for a fee. For any other than the most straightforward enquiries, it is better to write to a record office than to telephone and it is courteous to enclose a pre-paid envelope for a reply. An increasing number of offices provide a paid research service, the use of which is limited only by the client's resources.

The work can be slow and at times frustrating, but there are many exciting and satisfying moments. Each year tens of thousands of people get pleasure and fascination from using the marvellous heritage of records which we have in this country. With proper care and respect for the documents you too can benefit and, at the same time, ensure that future generations will also be able to enjoy the privilege.

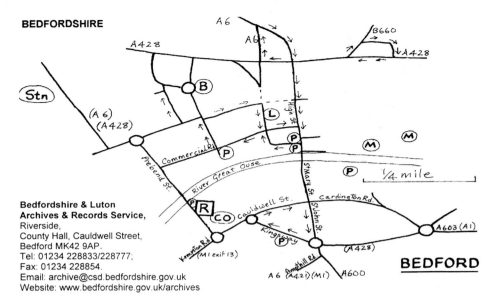

BEDFORDSHIRE

BEDFORD

Bedfordshire & Luton
Archives & Records Service,
Riverside,
County Hall, Cauldwell Street,
Bedford MK42 9AP.
Tel: 01234 228833/228777;
Fax: 01234 228854.
Email: archive@csd.bedfordshire.gov.uk
Website: www.bedfordshire.gov.uk/archives

No CARN ticket required;
no bookings system.

BERKSHIRE

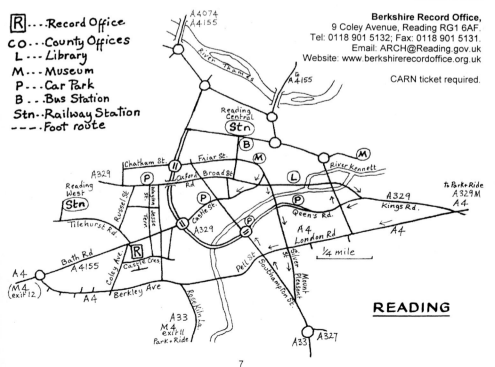

READING

R ... Record Office
CO ... County Offices
L ... Library
M ... Museum
P ... Car Park
B ... Bus Station
Stn ... Railway Station
---- Foot route

Berkshire Record Office,
9 Coley Avenue, Reading RG1 6AF.
Tel: 0118 901 5132; Fax: 0118 901 5131.
Email: ARCH@Reading.gov.uk
Website: www.berkshirerecordoffice.org.uk

CARN ticket required.

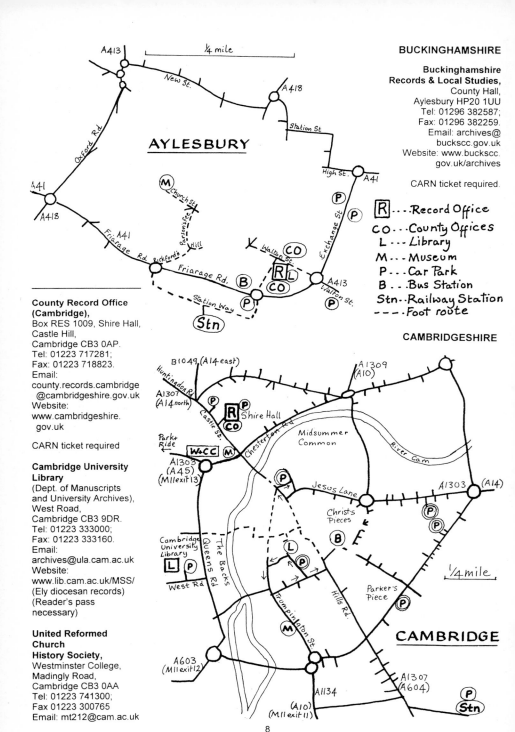

BUCKINGHAMSHIRE

Buckinghamshire Records & Local Studies,
County Hall,
Aylesbury HP20 1UU
Tel: 01296 382587;
Fax: 01296 382259.
Email: archives@
buckscc.gov.uk
Website: www.buckscc.
gov.uk/archives

CARN ticket required.

R ... Record Office
CO ... County Offices
L ... Library
M ... Museum
P ... Car Park
B ... Bus Station
Stn .. Railway Station
- - - - .. Foot route

CAMBRIDGESHIRE

County Record Office (Cambridge),
Box RES 1009, Shire Hall,
Castle Hill,
Cambridge CB3 0AP.
Tel: 01223 717281;
Fax: 01223 718823.
Email:
county.records.cambridge
@cambridgeshire.gov.uk
Website:
www.cambridgeshire.
gov.uk

CARN ticket required

Cambridge University Library
(Dept. of Manuscripts
and University Archives),
West Road,
Cambridge CB3 9DR.
Tel: 01223 333000;
Fax: 01223 333160.
Email:
archives@ula.cam.ac.uk
Website:
www.lib.cam.ac.uk/MSS/
(Ely diocesan records)
(Reader's pass
necessary)

United Reformed Church
History Society,
Westminster College,
Madingly Road,
Cambridge CB3 0AA
Tel: 01223 741300;
Fax 01223 300765
Email: mt212@cam.ac.uk

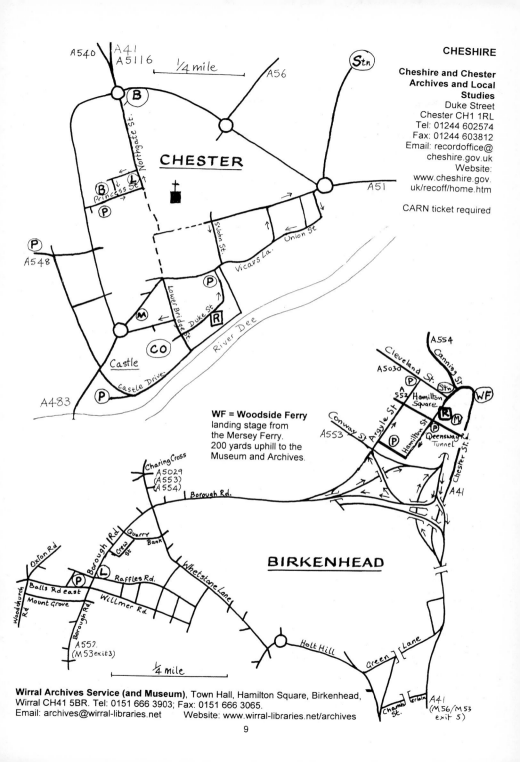

CHESHIRE

Cheshire and Chester Archives and Local Studies
Duke Street
Chester CH1 1RL
Tel: 01244 602574
Fax: 01244 603812
Email: recordoffice@
cheshire.gov.uk
Website:
www.cheshire.gov.
uk/recoff/home.htm

CARN ticket required

WF = Woodside Ferry landing stage from the Mersey Ferry. 200 yards uphill to the Museum and Archives.

Wirral Archives Service (and Museum), Town Hall, Hamilton Square, Birkenhead, Wirral CH41 5BR. Tel: 0151 666 3903; Fax: 0151 666 3065.
Email: archives@wirral-libraries.net   Website: www.wirral-libraries.net/archives

9

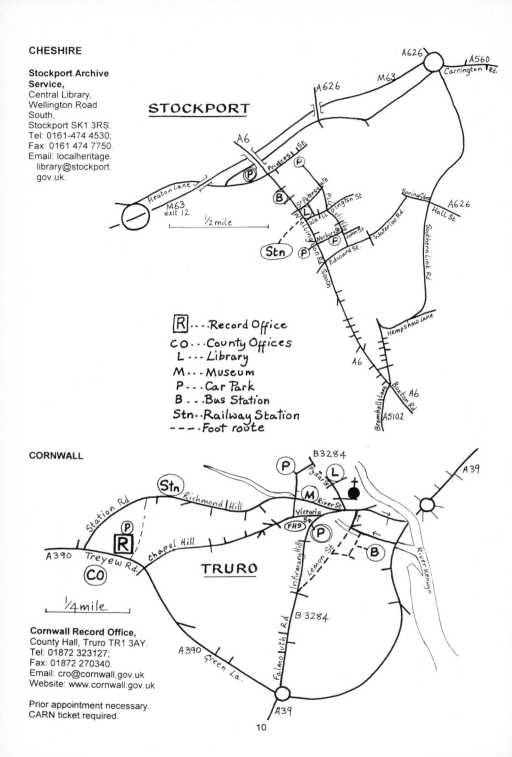

CHESHIRE

**Stockport Archive
Service,**
Central Library,
Wellington Road
South,
Stockport SK1 3RS.
Tel: 0161-474 4530;
Fax: 0161 474 7750.
Email: localheritage.
  library@stockport.
  gov.uk.

STOCKPORT

R ... Record Office
CO ... County Offices
L ... Library
M ... Museum
P ... Car Park
B ... Bus Station
Stn ... Railway Station
- - - ... Foot route

CORNWALL

TRURO

Cornwall Record Office,
County Hall, Truro TR1 3AY.
Tel: 01872 323127;
Fax: 01872 270340.
Email: cro@cornwall.gov.uk
Website: www.cornwall.gov.uk

Prior appointment necessary.
CARN ticket required.

CUMBERLAND

Cumbria Record Office (Carlisle),
The Castle, Carlisle CA3 8UR.
Tel: 01228 607285;
Fax: 01228 607270.
Email: carlisle.record.office@cumbriacc.gov.uk
Website: www.cumbria.gov.uk/archives

CARN ticket required.

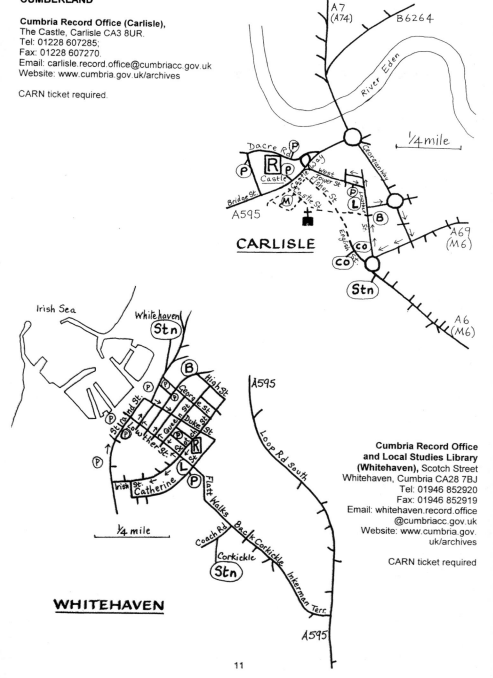

CARLISLE

WHITEHAVEN

**Cumbria Record Office
and Local Studies Library
(Whitehaven),** Scotch Street
Whitehaven, Cumbria CA28 7BJ
Tel: 01946 852920
Fax: 01946 852919
Email: whitehaven.record.office
@cumbriacc.gov.uk
Website: www.cumbria.gov.
uk/archives

CARN ticket required

DERBYSHIRE

Derbyshire Record Office,
Postal address:
County Hall, Matlock DE4 3AG.
Tel: 01629 585347 (searchroom);
Fax: 01629 57611.
Email: record.office@derbyshire.gov.uk
Actual location in Ernest Bailey
Building on New Street, Matlock, as shown.

MATLOCK

R ... Record Office
CO ... County Offices
L ... Library
M ... Museum
P ... Car Park
B ... Bus Station
Stn .. Railway Station
---- . Foot route

Not mapped:
Derby Library Local Studies Dept.,
25b Irongate, Derby DE1 3GL
Tel: 01332 255393.
Fax: 01332 255381.
Email: localstudies.library@derby.gov.uk
Website: www.derby.gov.uk/libraries/about/local_studies.htm

BARNSTAPLE

DEVON

North Devon Record Office,
North Devon Library and Record Office,
Tuly Street, Barnstaple EX31 1EL.
Tel/Fax: 01271 388608.
Website: www.devon.gov.uk/dro

CARN ticket required. Daily charge.

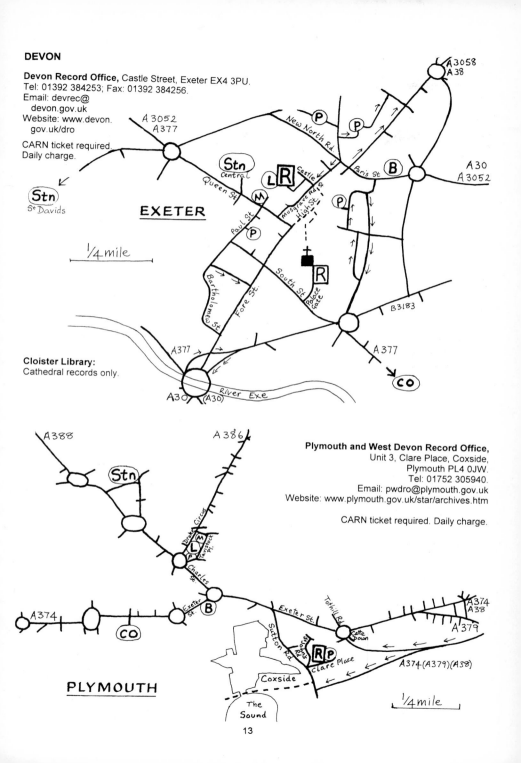

DEVON

Devon Record Office, Castle Street, Exeter EX4 3PU.
Tel: 01392 384253; Fax: 01392 384256.
Email: devrec@
  devon.gov.uk
Website: www.devon.
  gov.uk/dro

CARN ticket required.
Daily charge.

EXETER

1/4 mile

Cloister Library:
Cathedral records only.

Plymouth and West Devon Record Office,
Unit 3, Clare Place, Coxside,
Plymouth PL4 0JW.
Tel: 01752 305940.
Email: pwdro@plymouth.gov.uk
Website: www.plymouth.gov.uk/star/archives.htm

CARN ticket required. Daily charge.

PLYMOUTH

1/4 mile

DORSET

Dorset Record Office,
Bridport Road,
Dorchester DT1 1RP
Tel: 01305 250550;
Fax: 01305 257184.
Email: archives@
    dorset-cc.gov.uk
Website: www.dorset-cc.
    gov.uk/archives

Bus stops off High Street
Proof of I.D. required
Get permit for parking
from Dorset R.O.

R ... Record Office
CO ... County Offices
L ... Library
M ... Museum
P ... Car Park
B ... Bus Station
Stn .. Railway Station
---- . Foot route

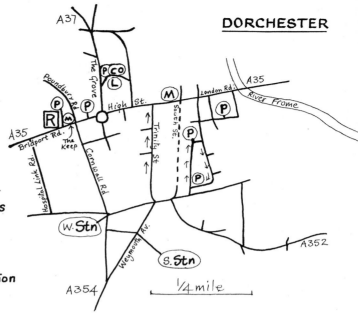

DORCHESTER

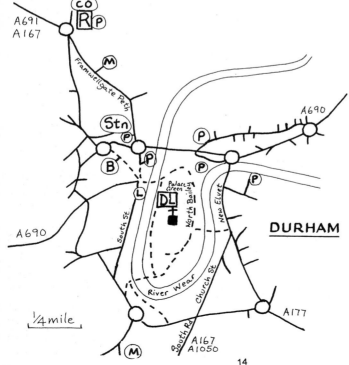

DURHAM

Co. DURHAM

**Durham County Record
Office,** County Hall
Durham DH1 5UL
Tel: 0191-383 3253 or
    0191-383 3474
Fax: 0191 383 4500
Email: record.office
    @durham.gov.uk
Website: www.durham.
    gov.uk/recordoffice

**DL = Durham University
Library Archives and
Special Collections**
Palace Green Section
Palace Green
Durham DH1 3RN
Tel: 0191-374 3001
Fax: 0191 374 3002
Email: pg.library@
    durham.ac.uk
Website: www.dur.ac.
    uk/library/asc/

Parking is very limited
on Palace Green

ESSEX

Essex Record Office
Wharf Road
Chelmsford CM2 6YT
Tel: 01245 244644
Fax: 01245 244655
Email: ero.enquiry@
essexcc.gov.uk
Website: www.essexcc.
gov.uk/ero

CARN ticket required.

SOUTHEND

CHELMSFORD

COLCHESTER

Essex Record Office
(Southend Branch)
Central Library, Victoria Avenue
Southend-on-Sea SS2 6EX
Tel: 01702 464278; Fax: 01702 464253
Email: ero.southend@essexcc.gov.uk
Website: www.essexcc.gov.uk/ero

CARN ticket required.

Essex Record Office
(Colchester & N.E. Essex Branch)
Stanwell House, Stanwell Street
Colchester, Essex CO2 7DL
Tel: 01206 572099; Fax: 01206 574541
Email: ero.colchester@essexcc.gov.uk
Website: www.essexcc.gov.uk/ero

CARN ticket required.

GLOUCESTERSHIRE and BRISTOL

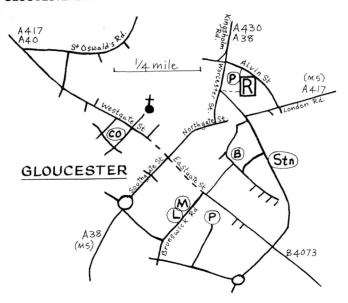

GLOUCESTER

Gloucestershire Record Office,
Clarence Row,
Alvin Street,
Gloucester GL1 3DW
Tel:01452 425295;
Fax: 01452 426378.
Email:
records@gloscc.gov.uk
Website:
archives.gloscc.gov.uk

Parking at the Record
Office, enter from
Alvin Street.
Access by footpath only
from Worcester Street.

Modern records are at
the Shire Hall (CO) for
which an appointment
must be made.

Gloucester Library,
Brunswick Road,
Gloucester GL1 1HT.
Tel: 01452 426979;
Fax: 01452 521468.
Email: localstudies@
gloscc.gov.uk
Website: gloscc.gov.
uk/libraries
For the 'Gloucester-
shire Collection'.

Bristol Record Office,
'B' Bond Warehouse, Smeaton Road,
Bristol BS1 6XN.
Tel: 0117 922 4224; Fax 0117 922 4236.
Email: bro@bristol-city.gov.uk
Website: www.bristol-city.gov.uk/recordoffice

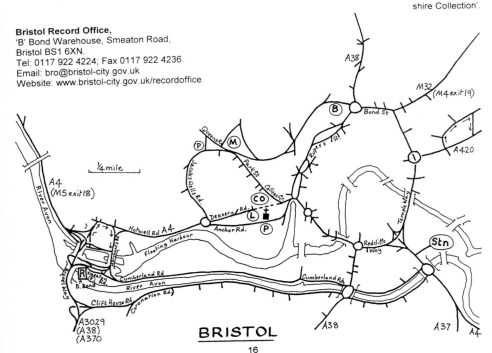

BRISTOL

WINCHESTER

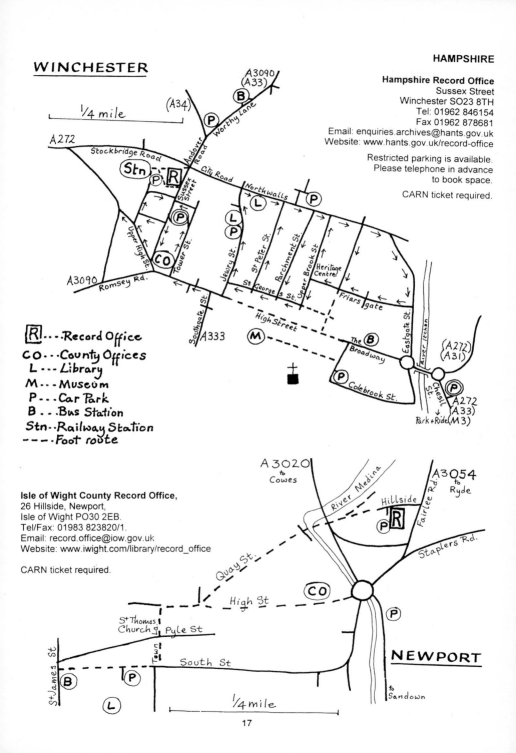

1/4 mile

A3090 (A33)
(A34)
A272
Stockbridge Road
A3090
Romsey Rd.
Andover Road
Worthy Lane
City Road
Sussex Street
Northwalls
St. Peter St.
Parchment St.
Upper Brook St.
Heritage Centre
Upper High St.
Tower St.
Jewry St.
St. George's St.
Southgate St.
A333
High Street
Friars gate
Eastgate St.
River Itchen
Chesil St.
The Broadway
Colebrook St.
Park + Ride (M3)
(A272) (A31)
A272 (A33)

R ... Record Office
CO ... County Offices
L ... Library
M ... Museum
P ... Car Park
B ... Bus Station
Stn .. Railway Station
---- Foot route

HAMPSHIRE

Hampshire Record Office
Sussex Street
Winchester SO23 8TH
Tel: 01962 846154
Fax 01962 878681
Email: enquiries.archives@hants.gov.uk
Website: www.hants.gov.uk/record-office

Restricted parking is available.
Please telephone in advance
to book space.

CARN ticket required.

Isle of Wight County Record Office,
26 Hillside, Newport,
Isle of Wight PO30 2EB.
Tel/Fax: 01983 823820/1.
Email: record.office@iow.gov.uk
Website: www.iwight.com/library/record_office

CARN ticket required.

A3020 to Cowes
River Medina
A3054 to Ryde
Hillside
Fairlee Rd.
Staplers Rd.
Quay St.
High St
CO
St Thomas Church
Pyle St
St James St
South St
B
L
NEWPORT
to Sandown
1/4 mile

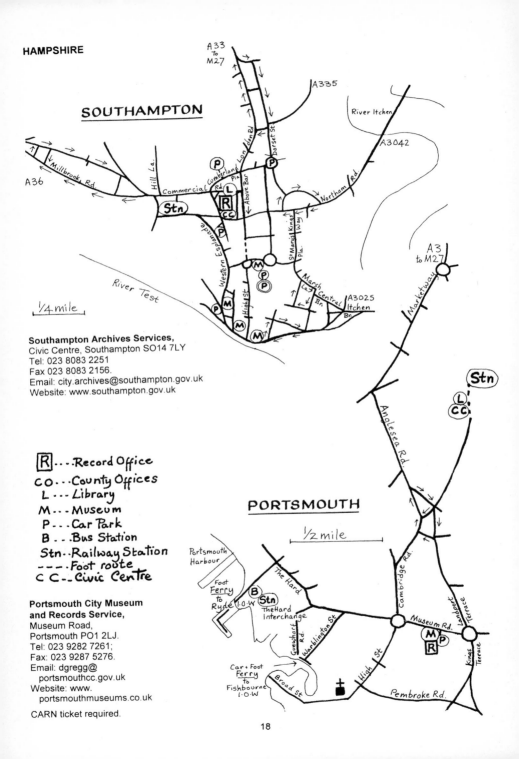

HAMPSHIRE

SOUTHAMPTON

A36

River Test

¼ mile

Southampton Archives Services,
Civic Centre, Southampton SO14 7LY
Tel: 023 8083 2251
Fax 023 8083 2156.
Email: city.archives@southampton.gov.uk
Website: www.southampton.gov.uk

R ... Record Office
CO ... County Offices
L ... Library
M ... Museum
P ... Car Park
B ... Bus Station
Stn ... Railway Station
--- Foot route
C C ... Civic Centre

**Portsmouth City Museum
and Records Service,**
Museum Road,
Portsmouth PO1 2LJ.
Tel: 023 9282 7261;
Fax: 023 9287 5276.
Email: dgregg@
    portsmouthcc.gov.uk
Website: www.
    portsmouthmuseums.co.uk

CARN ticket required.

PORTSMOUTH

½ mile

Portsmouth Harbour

Foot Ferry to Ryde I.O.W

Car + Foot Ferry to Fishbourne I.O.W

HEREFORDSHIRE

Herefordshire Record Office,
The Old Barracks,
Harold Street,
Hereford HR1 2QX.
Tel: 01432 260750;
Fax: 01432 260066.
Email: shubbard@
  herefordshire.gov.uk
Website: www.recordoffice.
  herefordshire.gov.uk

Car parking at the
Record Office.

CARN ticket required.

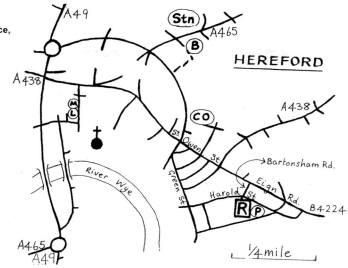

HERTFORDSHIRE

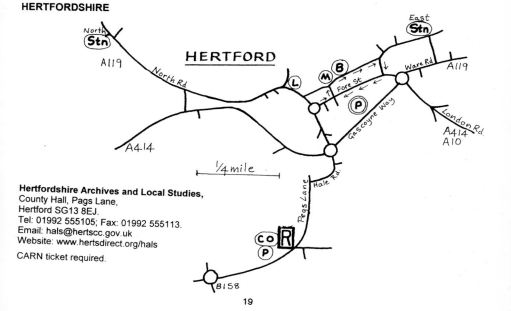

Hertfordshire Archives and Local Studies,
County Hall, Pags Lane,
Hertford SG13 8EJ.
Tel: 01992 555105; Fax: 01992 555113.
Email: hals@hertscc.gov.uk
Website: www.hertsdirect.org/hals

CARN ticket required.

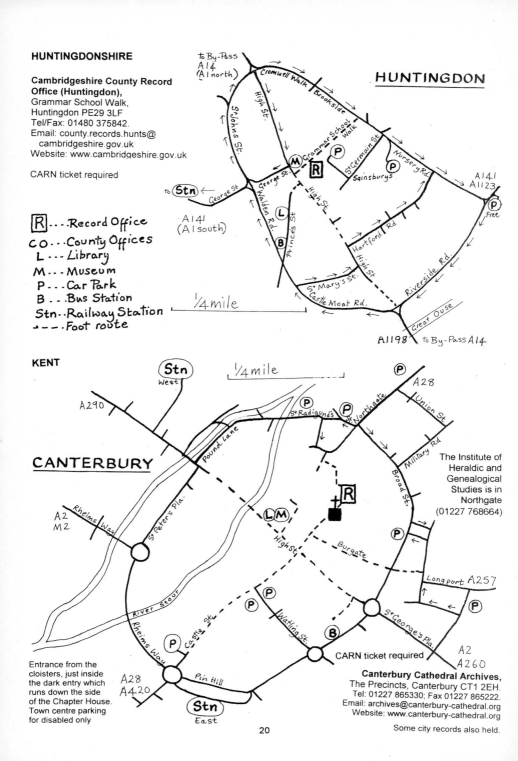

HUNTINGDONSHIRE

Cambridgeshire County Record Office (Huntingdon),
Grammar School Walk,
Huntingdon PE29 3LF
Tel/Fax: 01480 375842.
Email: county.records.hunts@
   cambridgeshire.gov.uk
Website: www.cambridgeshire.gov.uk

CARN ticket required

R ... Record Office
CO ... County Offices
L ... Library
M ... Museum
P ... Car Park
B ... Bus Station
Stn .. Railway Station
- - - . Foot route

¼ mile

HUNTINGDON

to By-Pass A14 (A1 north)
Cromwell Walk
Brookside
High St.
St Johns St.
Grammar School Walk
St Germain St.
Nursery Rd.
Sainsburys
A141 A1123
George St.
to Stn
George St.
Walden Rd.
High St.
Free
A141 (A1 south)
Princes St.
Hartford Rd.
High St.
St Mary's St.
Castle Moat Rd.
Riverside Rd.
Great Ouse
A1198   to By-Pass A14

KENT

Stn West
¼ mile
P A28
A290
Pound Lane
St Radigund's
St Northgate
Union St.

CANTERBURY

Military Rd.
Broad St.
St Peters Pla.
Rheims Way
A2 M2
LM
High St.
Burgate
Longport A257
River Stour
Watling St.
Castle St.
Rheims Way
Pin Hill
St George's Pla.
Stn East
A28 A420
A2 A260

The Institute of Heraldic and Genealogical Studies is in Northgate (01227 768664)

CARN ticket required

Entrance from the cloisters, just inside the dark entry which runs down the side of the Chapter House. Town centre parking for disabled only

Canterbury Cathedral Archives,
The Precincts, Canterbury CT1 2EH.
Tel: 01227 865330; Fax 01227 865222.
Email: archives@canterbury-cathedral.org
Website: www.canterbury-cathedral.org

Some city records also held.

20

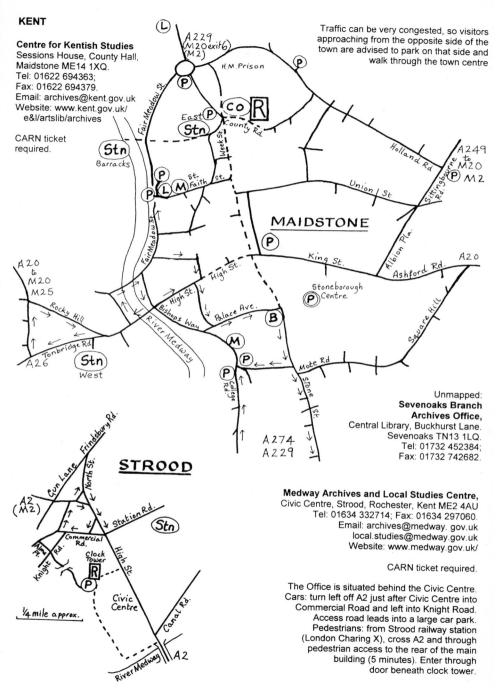

KENT

Centre for Kentish Studies
Sessions House, County Hall,
Maidstone ME14 1XQ.
Tel: 01622 694363;
Fax: 01622 694379.
Email: archives@kent.gov.uk
Website: www.kent.gov.uk/
 e&l/artslib/archives

CARN ticket
required.

Traffic can be very congested, so visitors
approaching from the opposite side of the
town are advised to park on that side and
walk through the town centre

Unmapped:
**Sevenoaks Branch
Archives Office,**
Central Library, Buckhurst Lane.
Sevenoaks TN13 1LQ.
Tel: 01732 452384;
Fax: 01732 742682.

Medway Archives and Local Studies Centre,
Civic Centre, Strood, Rochester, Kent ME2 4AU
Tel: 01634 332714; Fax: 01634 297060.
Email: archives@medway. gov.uk
local.studies@medway.gov.uk
Website: www.medway.gov.uk/

CARN ticket required.

The Office is situated behind the Civic Centre.
Cars: turn left off A2 just after Civic Centre into
Commercial Road and left into Knight Road.
Access road leads into a large car park.
Pedestrians: from Strood railway station
(London Charing X), cross A2 and through
pedestrian access to the rear of the main
building (5 minutes). Enter through
door beneath clock tower.

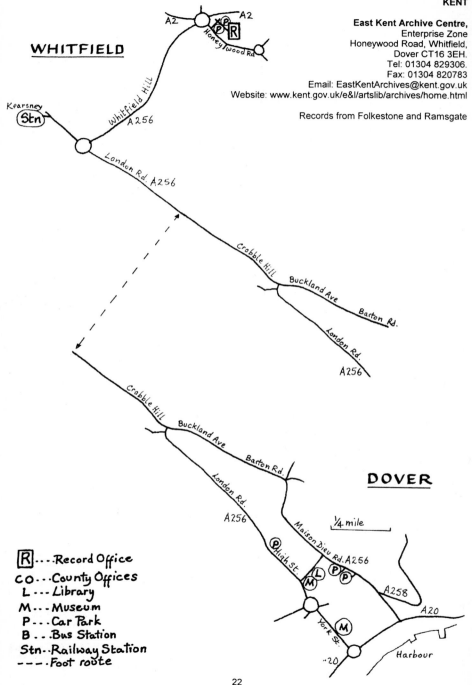

KENT

East Kent Archive Centre,
Enterprise Zone
Honeywood Road, Whitfield,
Dover CT16 3EH.
Tel: 01304 829306.
Fax: 01304 820783
Email: EastKentArchives@kent.gov.uk
Website: www.kent.gov.uk/e&l/artslib/archives/home.html

Records from Folkestone and Ramsgate

WHITFIELD

DOVER

¼ mile

R ··· Record Office
CO ··· County Offices
L ··· Library
M ··· Museum
P ··· Car Park
B ·· Bus Station
Stn ·· Railway Station
---- Foot route

22

LANCASHIRE

Lancashire Record Office,
Bow Lane, Preston PR1 2RE
Tel: 01772 263039;
Fax: 01772 263050.
Email: record.office@
ed.lancscc.gov.uk
Website: www.lancashire.gov.
uk/education/lifelong/
recordindex.shtm

CARN ticket required.

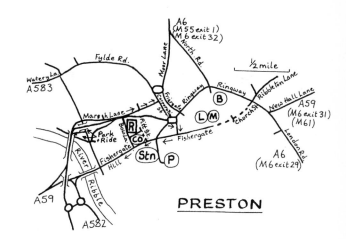

Cumbria Record Office, Barrow
140 Duke Street,
Barrow-in-Furness LA14 1XW.
Tel: 01229 894377;
Fax: 01229 894364.
Email: barrow.record.office@
cumbriacc.gov.uk

CARN ticket required.

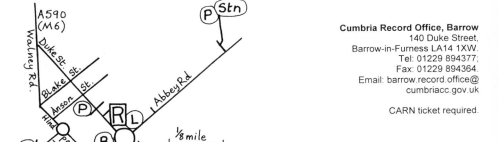

Wigan Archives Service
Wigan Record Office, Town Hall,
Leigh, Lancs. WN7 2DY.
Tel: 01942 404431; Fax: 01942 404425.
Email: heritage@wiganmbc.gov.uk
Website: www.wiganmbc.gov.uk

LANCASHIRE

MANCHESTER

Greater Manchester County Record Office,
56 Marshall Street, New Cross,
Manchester M4 5FU.
Tel: 0161-832 5284; Fax 0161 839 3808.
Email: archives@gmcro.co.uk
Website: www.gmcro-co.uk

CARN ticket required.

Manchester Archives Unit, Central Library,
St. Peter's Square, Manchester M2 5PD.
Tel: 0161-234 1980 (archives), 1979 (local studies);
Fax 0161 234 1927.
Email: archives@libraries.manchester.gov.uk
Website: www.manchester.gov.uk/libraries/arls

John Rylands University Library of Manchester,
150 Deansgate, Manchester M3 3EH.
Tel: 0161-834 5343;
Fax 0161 834 5574.
Email: spcoll72@fs1.li.man.ac.uk
Website: www.rylibweb.man.ac.uk/spcollcat

The People's History Museum (MLH),
Labour History Archive & Study Centre
(managed by University of Manchester),
103 Princess Street, Manchester M1 6DD.
Tel: 0161-228 7212;
Fax 0161 237 5965.
Email: lhasc@fs1.li.man.ac.uk
Website as John Rylands University Library.

LANCASHIRE

Not mapped:

Bolton Archive and Local Studies Service,
Central Library, Le Mans Crescent, Bolton BL1 1SE.
Tel: 01204 332185; Fax 01204 332225.
Email: archives.library@bolton.gov.uk

Bury Archive Service (behind the Derby
Hall), Edwin Street (off Crompton Street),
Bury BL9 0AS. Tel: 0161-797 6697.
Email: information@bury.gov.uk
Website: www.bury.gov.uk/
(intending users should write beforehand
for precise location map)

Rochdale Libraries (Local Studies),
3rd floor, Champneys Hall,
Drake Street, Rochdale OL16 1PB
Tel: 01706 864915.
Email:localstudies@rochdale.gov.uk
Moving late 2002 to
Touchstones, The Esplanade,
Rochdale OL16 1AQ.

Tameside Archive Service, Local Studies Library,
Astley Cheetham Public Library, Trinity St.,
Stalybridge SK15 2BN.
Tel: 0161-303 7937; Fax 0161 303 8289.
Email: localstudies.library@mail.tameside.gov.uk
Website: www.tameside.uk

Salford Local History Library
Salford Museum and Art Gallery,
Peel Park, Crescent,
Salford M5 4WU.
Tel: 0161-736 2649.
(this houses the city archives formerly held at
the now closed Salford Archives Centre at Irlam)

[R]...Record Office.
CO...County Offices
L...Library
M...Museum
P...Car Park
B...Bus Station
Stn..Railway Station
----.Foot route

**National Museums & Galleries
on Merseyside (N.M.G.M.),
Maritime Records Centre,**
Merseyside Maritime Museum,
Albert Dock, Liverpool L3 4AQ.
Tel: 0151-207 0001 ext 4424;
Fax: 0151 478 4590.
Email: maritime.archives@
nmgm.org.uk
Website: www.nmgm.org.uk

**Liverpool Record Office &
Local History Service**
Central Library
William Brown Street
Liverpool L3 8EW
Tel: 0151-233 5817
Fax: 0151 207 1342
Email:
recoffice.central.library@
liverpool.gov.uk

Corporation records;
parish registers; census;
directories; newspapers.

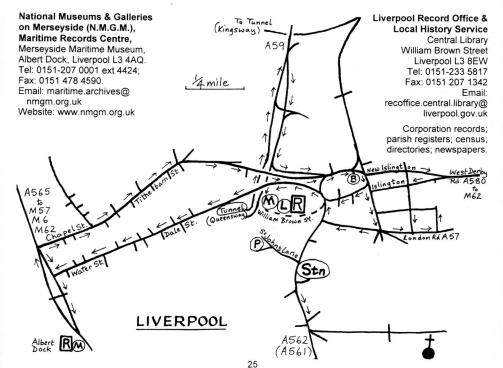

LIVERPOOL

25

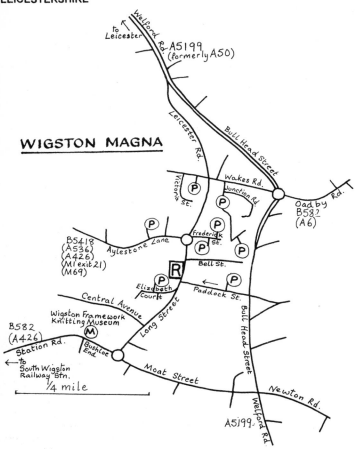

WIGSTON MAGNA

**The Record Office for Leicestershire,
Leicester and Rutland,**
Long Street, Wigston Magna,
Leicester LE18 2AH.
Tel: 0116 257 1080; Fax 0116 257 1120.
Email: recordoffice@leics.gov.uk

Wigston is about 4 miles from the centre of
Leicester reached by the A50 Welford Road
or from M1 junction 21.
Midland Fox bus service from St. Margaret's
bus station and from Charles Street via
Welford Road/Welford Place.
All services pass South Wigston station.

CARN ticket required

LINCOLNSHIRE

Lincolnshire Archives,
St. Rumbold Street, Lincoln LN2 5AB.
Tel: 01522 526204 [general enquiries];
01522 525158 [searchroom bookings];
Fax: 01522 530047.
Email: lincolnshire.archive@
 lincolnshire.gov.uk
Website: www.lincolnshire.gov.
 uk/archives

Special reader's pass *with photo* required;
CARN tickets *not* accepted.

Please make an appointment.
Own car park at rear of building (access
via Rosemary Lane off Monks Road).

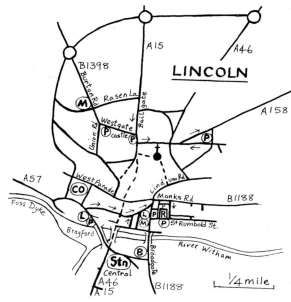

North East Lincolnshire Archives,
Town Hall, Town Hall Square,
Grimsby DN31 1HX
Tel: 01472 323585;
Fax: 01472 323582.
Email: john.wilson@nelincs.gov.uk

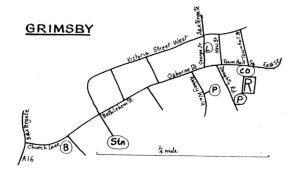

R ··· Record Office
CO ··· County Offices
L ··· Library
M ··· Museum
P ··· Car Park
B ··· Bus Station
Stn ··· Railway Station
- - - - Foot route

LONDON

Key

14 **Bank of England Archive;** Archive Section HO-SV, The Bank of England, Threadneedle Street, EC2R 8AH. Tel: 020-7601 4889/7601 5096; Fax 020-7601 4356.
Email: archive@bankofengland.co.uk   Website: www.bankofengland.co.uk

1 **British Library, Manuscripts Collections,** 96 Euston Road, NW1 2DB.
Tel: 020-7412 7513; Fax: 020-7412 7745.
Email: mss@bl.uk   Website: www.bl.uk/collections/manuscripts/

- **British Library Newspaper Library,** Colindale Avenue, London NW9 5HE. Tel: 020-7412 7353 (not mapped).

1 **B.L. Oriental & India Office Collections,** 96 Euston Road, NW1 2DB. Tel: 020-7412 7873;
Fax: 020-7412 7641.   Email: oioc-enquiries@bl.uk   Website: www.bl.uk/collections/oriental/

15 **College of Arms,** Queen Victoria Street, EC4V 4BT. Tel: 020-7248 2762; Fax: 020-7248 6448.
Email: enquiries@college-or-arms.gov.uk   Website: www.college-or-arms.gov.uk

13 **Corporation of London Records Office,** P.O. Box 270, Guildhall, EC2P 2EJ. Tel: 020-7332 1251;
Fax: 020-7710 8682. Email: clro@corpoflondon.gov.uk   Website: www.cityoflondon.gov.uk/archives/clro
(in North Office Block, immediately behind Guildhall, reached from Basinghall Street.)

3 **Family Records Centre,** 1 Myddelton Street, EC1R 1UW. Tel: 020-8392 5300 (general enquiries), 020-7233 9233
(certificate enquiries); Fax: 020-8392 5307.   Email: certificate.services@ons.gov.uk (certificate enquiries)
Website: www.pro.gov.uk/about/fre/   Postal enquiries for certificates to Smedley Hydro, Southport PR8 2HH.

12 **Guildhall Library,** Aldermanbury, EC2P 2EJ. Tel: 020-7332 1862/3; Fax: 020-7600 3384;
Email: manuscripts.guildhall@corpoflondon.gov.uk   Website: ihr.sas.ac.uk/gh/

18 **House of Lords Record Office (The Parliamentary Archives),** House of Lords, SW1A 0PW.
Tel: 020-7219 3074; Fax: 020-7219 2570.   Email: hlro@parliament.uk   Website:www.parliament.uk

20 **Lambeth Palace Library,** SE1 7JU. Tel: 020-7898 1400; Fax: 020-7928 7932.
Website: www.lambethpalacelibrary.org

6 **London Metropolitan Archives,** 40 Northampton Road, EC1R 0HB. Tel: 020-7332 3820;
Fax: 020-7833 9136. Email: lma@ms.corpoflondon.gov.uk   Website: www.cityoflondon.gov.uk/lma
Car parking, by prior arrangement, for disabled drivers only; N.C.P. adjacent (pricey).

5 **Post Office Archives and Record Centre,** Phoenix Place (near Freeling House, Mount Pleasant Sorting
Office), Farringdon Road, WC1X 0DL. Tel: 020-7239 2570; Fax: 020-7239 2576.
Email: heritage@consignia.com   Website: www.consignia.com/heritage

10 **The Principal Registry of the Family Division, Probate Department,**
1st Avenue House, 45-49 High Holborn, WC1V 6NP. Tel: 020-7947 6939.   Website: www.courtservice.gov.uk

11 **Royal Commission on Historical Manuscripts,** Quality House, Quality Court, Chancery Lane, WC2A 1HP.
Tel: 020-7242 1198; Fax: 020-7831 3550.   Email: nra@hmc.gov.uk   Website: www.hmc.gov.uk/
Housing the National Register of Archives, the Manorial Documents Register and the Tithe Documents Register.

2 **Religious Society of Friends' (Quakers) Library,** Friends House, 173-177 Euston Road, NW1 2BJ.
Tel: 020-7663 1135; Fax: 020-7663 1001.   Email: library@quaker.org.uk   Website: www.quaker.org.uk/

8 **Society of Genealogists,** 14 Charterhouse Buildings, Goswell Road, EC1M 7BA.
Tel: 020-7251 8799; Fax: 020-7250 1800.   Email: library@sog.org.uk   Website: www.sog.org.uk/
Charterhouse Buildings is a cul-de-sac, beside the National Westminster Bank, at the junction of Goswell Road
and Clerkenwell Road, about 500 yards north of Barbican station (on the Circle and Metropolitan underground
lines). Buses 4, 55, 56, 243 and 505 stop nearby.

- **United Reformed Church History Society.** Now located at Westminster College, Cambridge – see page 8.

17 **Westminster Abbey Muniment Room and Library,** SW1P 3PA. Tel: 020-7222 5152; Fax: 020-7654 4827
Email: library@westminster-abbey.org   Website: www.westminster-abbey.org/

19 **City of Westminster Archives Centre,** 10 St. Ann's Street, SW1P 2DE. Tel: 020-7641 5180; Fax: 020-7641 5179.
Email: archives@westminster.gov.uk   Website: www.westminster.gov.uk/archives

- **Westminster (Roman Catholic) Diocesan Archives,** 16a Abingdon Road, Kensington, W8 6AF.
Tel: 020-7938 3580 (not mapped).

7 **Dr Williams's Library,** 14 Gordon Square, WC1H 0AR. Tel: 020-7387 3727.   Email: enquiries@DWLib.co.uk

Note. Because of changes in location since this map was first prepared, some numbers are no longer included.

See:
London Local Archives: A Directory of Local Authority Record Offices and Libraries, ed. Carolynne Cotton, Greater London Archives Network, 4th ed., 1999, for addresses, location, opening hours and facilities, area covered, at such repositories.

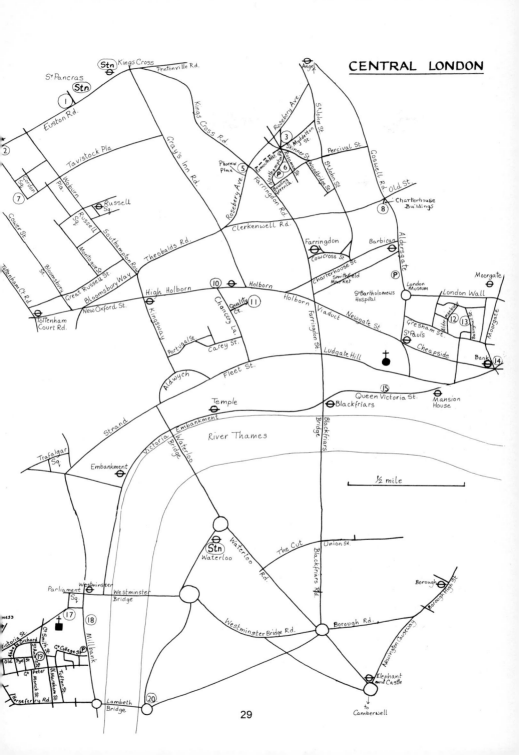

CENTRAL LONDON

29

LONDON

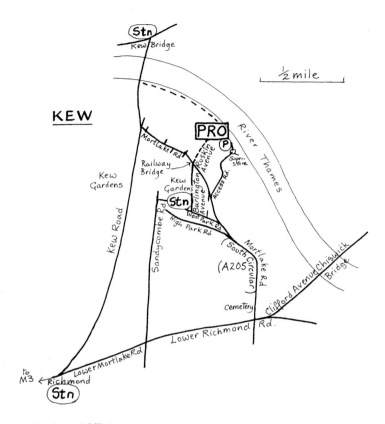

KEW

Public Record Office,
Ruskin Avenue, Kew, Richmond,
Surrey TW9 4DU.
Tel: 020 8876 3444;
Fax: 020 8878 8905.
Email: enquiry@pro.gov.uk
Website: www.pro.gov.uk/

If approaching from the north (Kew Bridge), the access road is on the left shortly beyond the railway bridge that crosses Mortlake Road (South Circular Road). At the mini roundabout on the access road, turn left, away from the shopping centre, and left again into the P.R.O. public car park. Pedestrian access from the car park and from Ruskin Avenue is along the path between the ponds. Look out for swans' droppings! All routes are clearly marked.

Coming by tube to Kew Gardens Station, set off along West Park Road opposite the station, and a sign pointing to the P.R.O. along Burlington Avenue is to be seen almost immediately. About ten minutes' walk.

LAMBETH & CAMBERWELL

Lambeth Archives Department
Minet Library
52 Knatchbull Road
London SE5 9QY
Tel: 020-7926 6076
Fax: 020 7926 6080
Email: jnewman@lambeth.gov.uk

½ mile

to Kennington Oval

to Kennington Oval

to Elephant & Castle

to Camberwell

Knatchbull Rd.

Camberwell New Rd

Camberwell Rd

Denmark Hill

L

Loughborough Rd

Minet Rd

Coldharbour Lane

Loughborough Rd

Loughborough Stn

to Blackfriars Station

Brixton Road

to Brixton

Cold harbour Lane

Acre Lane

R ···· Record Office
CO ··· County Offices
L ··· Library
M ··· Museum
P ··· Car Park
B ··· Bus Station
Stn·· Railway Station
---- Foot route

SUTTON

to Central London

Lodge Pl.

Lenham Rd

West St.

St Nicholas Way

High St.

Greyhound Rd.

Throwley Way

Gibson Rd.

St Nicholas Rd

Throwley Rd.

P

CO

L R

Carshalton Rd.

A232

Cheam Rd
A232
(A217n.)
A2043

Sutton Park Rd

Cheam Rd.

Safeway

P

Sutton Court Rd

Grove Rd.

Brighton Rd.

Stn

A217

¼ mile

Sutton Heritage Services,
Archive Section,
Archive & Local Studies Searchroom,
Central Library, St. Nicholas Way,
Sutton SM1 1EA.
Tel: 020 8770 4747; Fax: 020 8770 4777.
Email: local.studies@sutton.gov.uk
Website: www.sutton.gov.uk/

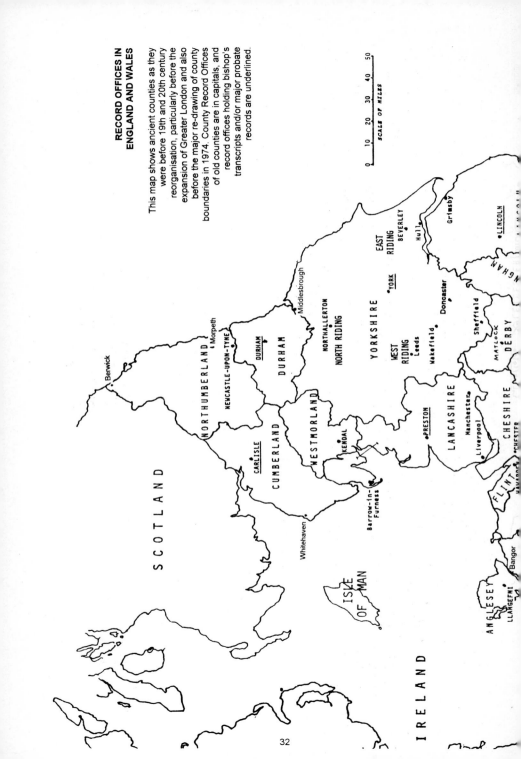

RECORD OFFICES IN
ENGLAND AND WALES

This map shows ancient counties as they
were before 19th and 20th century
reorganisation, particularly before the
expansion of Greater London and also
before the major re-drawing of county
boundaries in 1974. County Record Offices
of old counties are in capitals, and
record offices holding bishop's
transcripts and/or major probate
records are underlined.

SCALE OF MILES
0   10   20   30   40   50

SCOTLAND

IRELAND

ISLE OF MAN

Berwick

NORTHUMBERLAND
Morpeth
NEWCASTLE-UPON-TYNE

DURHAM
DURHAM

CUMBERLAND
CARLISLE

Whitehaven

WESTMORLAND
KENDAL

Barrow-in-Furness

Middlesbrough

NORTHALLERTON
NORTH RIDING

YORKSHIRE

EAST RIDING
BEVERLEY
Hull

York

WEST RIDING
Leeds
Wakefield
Doncaster
Sheffield

LANCASHIRE
PRESTON
Manchester
Liverpool

CHESHIRE
CHESTER

MATLOCK
DERBY

Grimsby

LINCOLN

ANGLESEY
LLANGEFNI

Bangor

FLINT

32

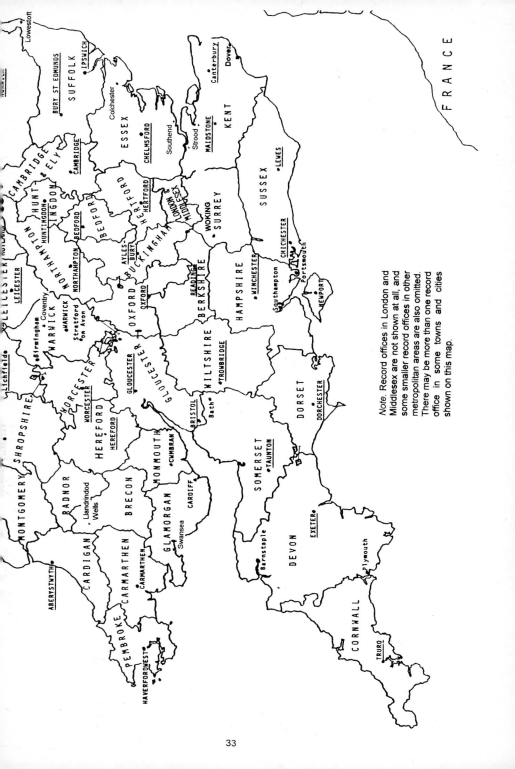

Note. Record offices in London and Middlesex are not shown at all, and some smaller record offices in other metropolitan areas are also omitted. There may be more than one record office in some towns and cities shown on this map.

FRANCE

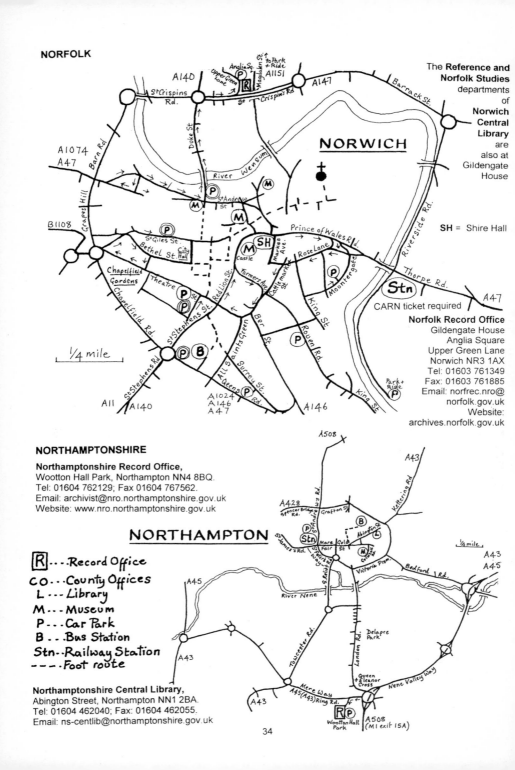

NORFOLK

A140

St Crispins Rd.

Anglia Sq.
Magdalen St.
to Park + Ride
Upper Green Lane

A1151

A147

Barrack St.

The **Reference and Norfolk Studies** departments of **Norwich Central Library** are also at Gildengate House

Duke St.

A1074
A47

Barn Rd.

River Wensum

NORWICH

Riverside Rd.

B1108

Grapes Hill

St Andrews St.

St Giles St.

Bethel St. City Hall

Prince of Wales Rd.

Rose Lane

Thorpe Rd.

A47

SH = Shire Hall

Chapelfield Gardens

Theatre St.

Castle

Market Ave.

Castle Mall

Farmers Ave.

Castle Meadow

Mountergate

Stn

CARN ticket required

Chapelfield Rd.

St Stephens St.

Red Lion St.

All Saints Green

Surrey St.

Ber St.

King St.

Raven Rd.

Norfolk Record Office
Gildengate House
Anglia Square
Upper Green Lane
Norwich NR3 1AX
Tel: 01603 761349
Fax: 01603 761885
Email: norfrec.nro@
norfolk.gov.uk
Website:
archives.norfolk.gov.uk

¼ mile

St Stephens Rd.

A1024
A146
A47

Queens Rd.

A146

King St.

Park + Ride

A11 A140

NORTHAMPTONSHIRE

Northamptonshire Record Office,
Wootton Hall Park, Northampton NN4 8BQ.
Tel: 01604 762129; Fax 01604 767562.
Email: archivist@nro.northamptonshire.gov.uk
Website: www.nro.northamptonshire.gov.uk

A508

A43

A428

Spencer Bridge Rd.

Grafton St.

Kettering Rd.

NORTHAMPTON

St James's Rd.

St Andrews Rd.

Stn

Mare Fair

Gold St.

Abington St.

B

L

M

¼ mile

A43
A45

St Peters Way

Victoria Prom.

Bedford Rd.

[R] ... Record Office
CO ... County Offices
L ... Library
M ... Museum
P ... Car Park
B ... Bus Station
Stn ... Railway Station
- - - - Foot route

A45

River Nene

Towcester Rd.

London Rd.

Delapre Park

Queen + Eleanor Cross

Nene Valley Way

A43

Mere Way
A45(A43) Ring Rd.

A43

RP
Wootton Hall Park

A508
(M1 exit 15A)

Northamptonshire Central Library,
Abington Street, Northampton NN1 2BA.
Tel: 01604 462040; Fax: 01604 462055.
Email: ns-centlib@northamptonshire.gov.uk

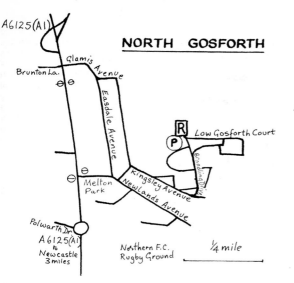

NORTH GOSFORTH

A6125(A1)
Glamis Avenue
Brunton La.
Easdale Avenue
Melton Park
Kingsley Avenue
Newlands Avenue
Low Gosforth Court
Brandling Drive
R P
Polwarth Dr.
A6125(A1)
to
Newcastle
3 miles
Northern F.C.
Rugby Ground
¼ mile

NORTHUMBERLAND

Northumberland Record Office,
Melton Park, North Gosforth,
Newcastle upon Tyne NE3 5QX.
Tel: 0191-236 2680; Fax 0191 217 0905.

Northumbria buses (from Haymarket
Bus Station - see below):
41-45 to Melton Park; **46** to Polwarth Drive.

From railway station, take Metro
to Regent Centre, then buses

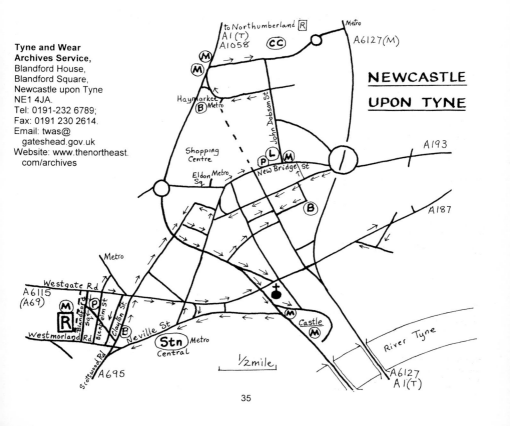

NEWCASTLE UPON TYNE

to Northumberland
A1(T)
A1058
CC
Metro
A6127(M)
M M
Haymarket B Metro
John Dobson St.
A193
Shopping Centre
P L M
Eldon Metro
Sq.
New Bridge St
B
A187
Metro
Westgate Rd
A6115 (A69)
M R
P
Clayton St
Neville St
B
Westmorland Rd
Scotswood Rd
A695
Stn Metro
Central
Castle
M
River Tyne
A6127
A1(T)
½ mile

Tyne and Wear Archives Service,
Blandford House,
Blandford Square,
Newcastle upon Tyne
NE1 4JA.
Tel: 0191-232 6789;
Fax: 0191 230 2614.
Email: twas@
  gateshead.gov.uk
Website: www.thenortheast.
  com/archives

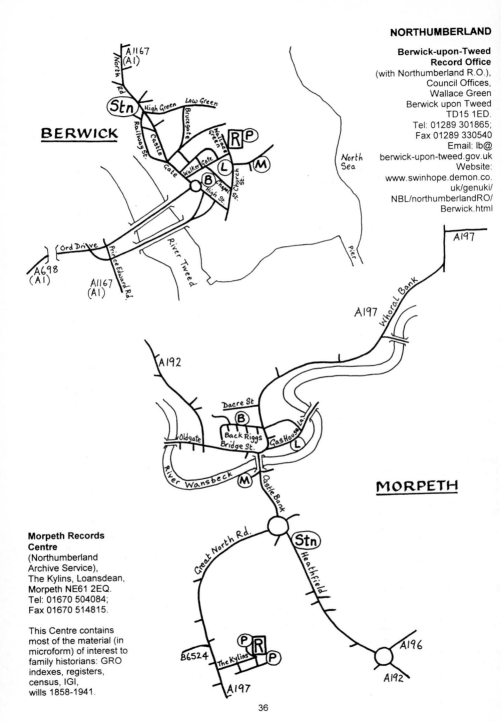

NORTHUMBERLAND

**Berwick-upon-Tweed
Record Office**
(with Northumberland R.O.),
Council Offices,
Wallace Green
Berwick upon Tweed
TD15 1ED.
Tel: 01289 301865;
Fax 01289 330540
Email: lb@
berwick-upon-tweed.gov.uk
Website:
www.swinhope.demon.co.
uk/genuki/
NBL/northumberlandRO/
Berwick.html

BERWICK

MORPETH

**Morpeth Records
Centre**
(Northumberland
Archive Service),
The Kylins, Loansdean,
Morpeth NE61 2EQ.
Tel: 01670 504084;
Fax 01670 514815.

This Centre contains
most of the material (in
microform) of interest to
family historians: GRO
indexes, registers,
census, IGI,
wills 1858-1941.

NOTTINGHAMSHIRE

Nottinghamshire Archives,
County House, Castle Meadow Road,
Nottingham NG2 1AG.
Tel: 0115 958 1634; Fax 0115 941 3997.
Email: archives@nottscc.gov.uk
Website: www.nottscc.gov.uk/libraries/archives

CARN ticket required.

Not mapped:
Nottingham University
Department of Manuscripts and Special Collections
Hallward Library, University Park, Nottingham NG7 2RD.
Tel: 0115-951 4565; Fax: 0115 951 4558.
Email: mss-library@nottingham.ac.uk
Website: mss.library.nottingham.ac.uk

Southwell Minster Library
Holds original Bishop's Transcripts for
Southwell Diocese

R .... Record Office
CO ... County Offices
L ... Library
M ... Museum
P ... Car Park
B .. Bus Station
Stn .. Railway Station
---- Foot route

OXFORDSHIRE

Centre for Oxfordshire Studies, Central Library, Westgate, Oxford OX1 1DJ.
Tel: 01865 815749.
Email: cos@oxfordshire.gov.uk

Charge for advance booking of microform readers.

Park and Ride bus service operates on A34 approach from north and south; and A40 (east)/A420 (west)

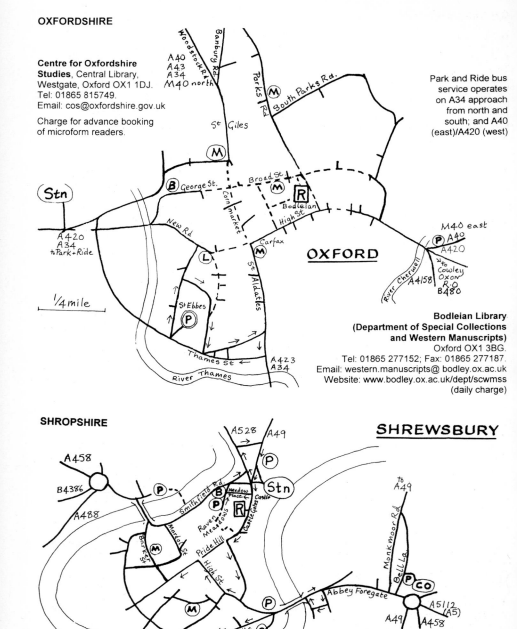

Bodleian Library
(Department of Special Collections and Western Manuscripts)
Oxford OX1 3BG.
Tel: 01865 277152; Fax: 01865 277187.
Email: western.manuscripts@ bodley.ox.ac.uk
Website: www.bodley.ox.ac.uk/dept/scwmss
(daily charge)

SHROPSHIRE

Shropshire Records and Research Centre
Castle Gates, Shrewsbury SY1 2AQ.
Tel: 01743 255350; Fax 01743 255355.
Email: research@shropshire-cc.gov.uk
Website: www.shropshire-cc.gov.uk/research.nsf

OXFORDSHIRE

Oxfordshire Record Office,
St. Luke's Church, Temple Road,
Cowley, Oxford OX4 2EX.
Tel: 01865 398200.
Email: archives@oxfordshire.gov.uk
Website: www.oxfordshire.gov.uk/cshaindx

CARN ticket required.
Prior notice needed for Oxford City archives.
Charge for advance booking of microform readers.
Small car park at record office.

R ··· Record Office
CO ··· County Offices
L ··· Library
M ··· Museum
P ··· Car Park
B ··· Bus Station
Stn ··· Railway Station
---- · Foot route

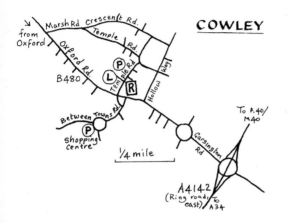

COWLEY

SOMERSET

Somerset Archive and Record Service,
Obridge Road, Taunton TA2 7PU.
Tel: 01823 278805/337600 (appointments).
Fax 01823 325402;
Email: archives@somerset.gov.uk
Website: www.somerset.gov.uk/archives

CARN ticket required.

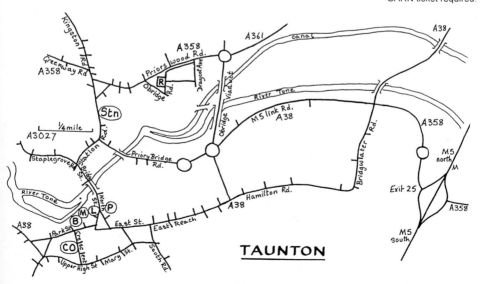

TAUNTON

SOMERSET

**Bath & North East Somerset
Record Office,**
Guildhall, Bath BA1 5AW.
Tel: 01225 477421;
Fax 01225 477439.
Email: archives@bathnes.gov.uk
Website: batharchives.co.uk

BATH

STAFFORDSHIRE

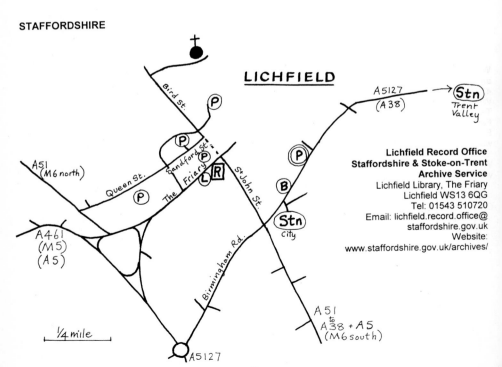

LICHFIELD

**Lichfield Record Office
Staffordshire & Stoke-on-Trent
Archive Service**
Lichfield Library, The Friary
Lichfield WS13 6QG
Tel: 01543 510720
Email: lichfield.record.office@
staffordshire.gov.uk
Website:
www.staffordshire.gov.uk/archives/

STAFFORDSHIRE

**Staffordshire Record Office,
Staffordshire & Stoke-on-Trent
Archive Service**
Eastgate Street
Stafford ST16 2LZ
Tel: 01785 278379;
Fax 01785 278384
Email: staffordshire.record.office@
staffordshire.gov.uk
Website:
www.staffordshire.gov.uk/archives/

William Salt Library
Eastgate Street
(adjacent to the Record
Office)
Tel: 01785 278372

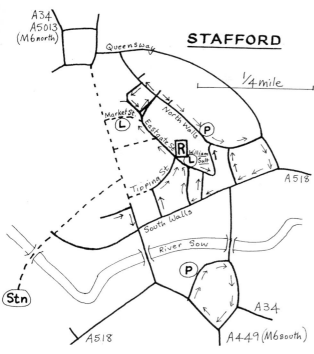

R ... Record Office
CO ... County Offices
L ... Library
M ... Museum
P ... Car Park
B ... Bus Station
Stn .. Railway Station
- - - - .. Foot route

**Wolverhampton Archives
and Local Studies,**
42-50 Snow Hill,
Wolverhampton WV2 4AG
Tel: 01902 552480;
Fax: 01902 552481.
Email:
wolverhamptonarchives@
dial.pipex.com
Website:
www.wolverhampton.gov.
uk/archives.htm

CARN ticket required.

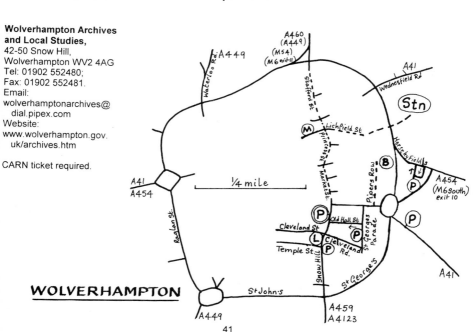

STAFFORDSHIRE

**Dudley Archives and
Local History Service,**
Mount Pleasant Street,
Coseley,
West Midlands WV14 9JR.
Tel/Fax: 01384 812770.
Email:
archives.pls@mbc.dudley.gov.uk
Website: www.dudley.gov.uk

Coseley is about two
miles north of Dudley
 town centre.
Now signed from
Ivyhouse Lane on A4123.

Walsall Archives Service,
Local History Centre,
Essex Street, Walsall WS2 7AS.
Tel: 01922 721305;
Fax: 01922 634954.
Email: localhistorycentre@walsall.gov.uk
Website: www.walsall.gov.uk

R ... Record Office
CO ... County Offices
L ... Library
M ... Museum
P ... Car Park
B ... Bus Station
Stn ... Railway Station
---- Foot route

Priory Road
and Tipton Road
lead to Dudley
town centre

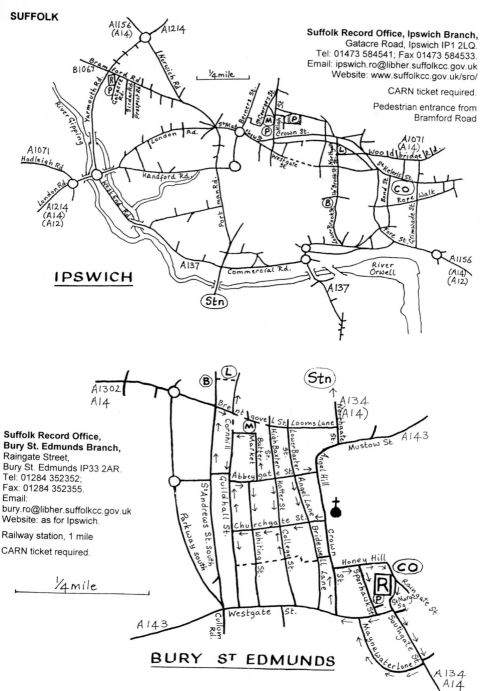

SUFFOLK

Suffolk Record Office, Ipswich Branch,
Gatacre Road, Ipswich IP1 2LQ.
Tel: 01473 584541; Fax 01473 584533.
Email: ipswich.ro@libher.suffolkcc.gov.uk
Website: www.suffolkcc.gov.uk/sro/

CARN ticket required.

Pedestrian entrance from
Bramford Road

IPSWICH

Suffolk Record Office,
Bury St. Edmunds Branch,
Raingate Street,
Bury St. Edmunds IP33 2AR.
Tel: 01284 352352;
Fax: 01284 352355.
Email:
bury.ro@libher.suffolkcc.gov.uk
Website: as for Ipswich.

Railway station, 1 mile

CARN ticket required.

BURY ST EDMUNDS

SUFFOLK

Suffolk Record Office, Lowestoft Branch,
Central Library, Clapham Road,
Lowestoft NR32 1DR.
Tel: 01502 405357; Fax 01502 405350;
Email: lowestoft.ro@libher.suffolkcc.gov.uk
Website: www.suffolkcc.gov.uk/sro/

CARN ticket required.

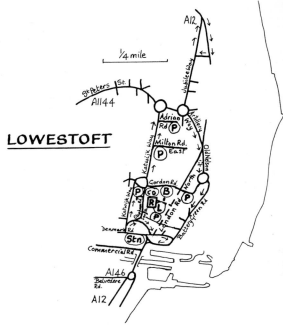

SURREY

Surrey History Centre
130 Goldsworth Road, Woking
Surrey GU21 6ND
Tel: 01483 594594
Fax: 01483 594595
Email: shs@surreycc.gov.uk
Website: www.shs.surreycc.gov.uk/

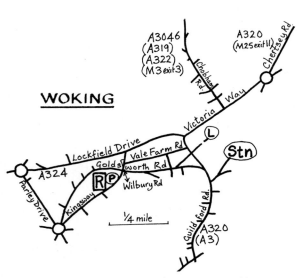

SUSSEX

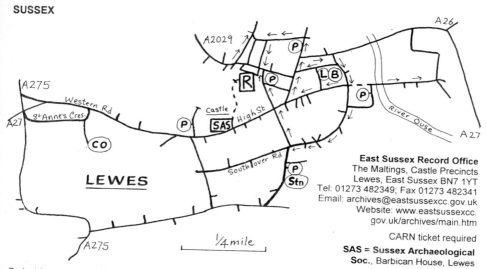

East Sussex Record Office
The Maltings, Castle Precincts
Lewes, East Sussex BN7 1YT
Tel: 01273 482349; Fax 01273 482341
Email: archives@eastsussexcc.gov.uk
Website: www.eastsussexcc.
gov.uk/archives/main.htm

CARN ticket required

**SAS = Sussex Archaeological
Soc.**, Barbican House, Lewes

Pedestrian access to The Maltings from the High Street is via the Castle Gate (through the Barbican Arch and past the Bowling Green). Parking at The Maltings is restricted to deliveries and disabled drivers; the nearest street parking is off the Offham Road (A2029) (about 5 minutes' walk) or use North Street pay car park.

West Sussex Record Office,
Sherburne House, 3 Orchard Street,
Chichester.
Tel: 01243 753600; Fax 01243 533959;
Email: records.office@westsussex.gov.uk
Website: www.westsussex.gov.uk/ro/

Postal enquiries:
West Sussex Record Office,
County Hall, Chichester PO19 1RN.

CARN ticket required.

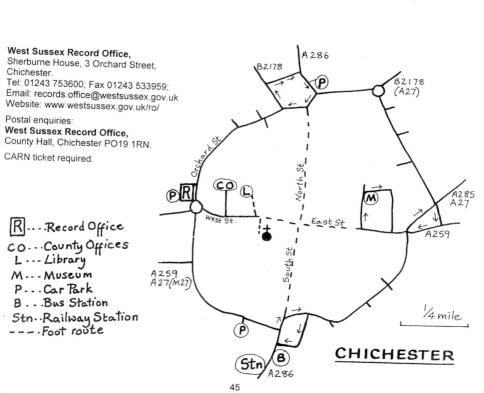

R . . . Record Office
CO . . . County Offices
L . . . Library
M . . . Museum
P . . . Car Park
B . . . Bus Station
Stn . . Railway Station
- - - . Foot route

WARWICKSHIRE

Warwick County Record Office,
Priory Park, Cape Road,
Warwick CV34 4JS.
Tel: 01926 412735;
Fax: 01926 412509.
Email: recordoffice@
warwickshire.gov.uk
Website:
www.warwickshire.gov.uk/
countyrecordoffice

The approach is by a drive off
Cape Road.

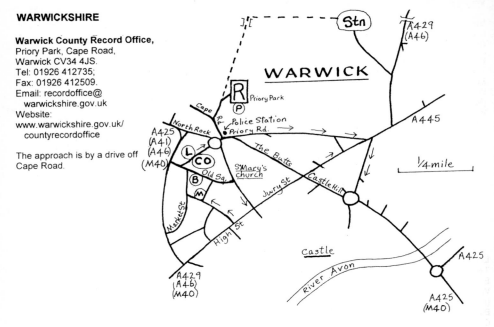

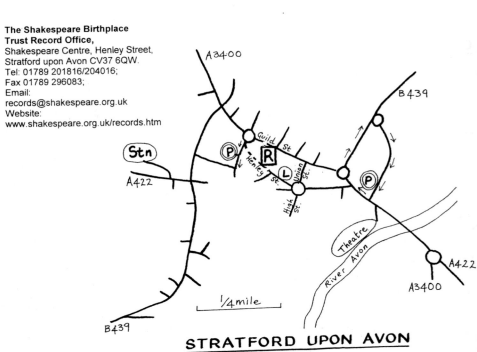

**The Shakespeare Birthplace
Trust Record Office,**
Shakespeare Centre, Henley Street,
Stratford upon Avon CV37 6QW.
Tel: 01789 201816/204016;
Fax 01789 296083;
Email:
records@shakespeare.org.uk
Website:
www.shakespeare.org.uk/records.htm

46

WARWICKSHIRE

Birmingham Central Library,
Chamberlain Square,
Birmingham B3 3HQ

Birmingham City Archives
Tel: 0121 303 4217; Fax 0121 464 1176.
Email: archives@birmingham.gov.uk
Website: www.birmingham.gov.uk/libraries
(MSS & archives for Birmingham,
Warwicks., Worcs., Staffs.)

CARN ticket required.

Local Studies and History Section
Tel: 0121-303 4549; Fax: 0121 464 0993.
Email: local.studies.library@birmingham.gov.uk
Website: www.birmingham.gov.uk
(printed material, census microfilm:
Birmingham and West Midlands
County, IGI, GRO indexes)

COVENTRY

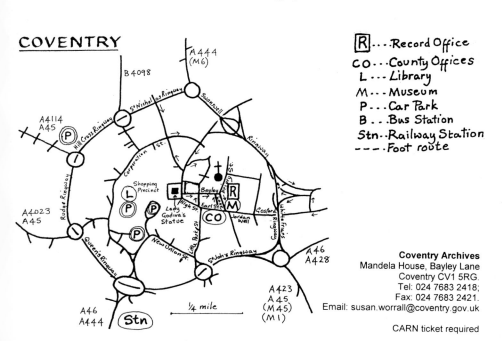

R ...Record Office
CO ...County Offices
L ...Library
M ...Museum
P ...Car Park
B ...Bus Station
Stn ..Railway Station
- - - .Foot route

Coventry Archives
Mandela House, Bayley Lane
Coventry CV1 5RG.
Tel: 024 7683 2418;
Fax: 024 7683 2421.
Email: susan.worrall@coventry.gov.uk

CARN ticket required

WESTMORLAND

Cumbria Record Office (Kendal),
County Offices, Kendal LA9 4RQ.
Tel: 01539 773540; Fax: 01539 773438.
Email: kendal.record.office@cumbriacc.gov.uk

CARN ticket required.

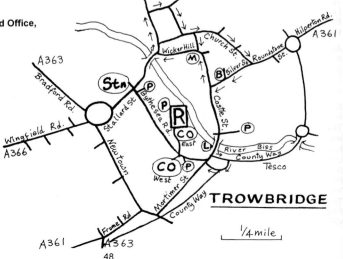

KENDAL

R ... Record Office
CO ... County Offices
L ... Library
M ... Museum
P ... Car Park
B ... Bus Station
Stn .. Railway Station
---- . Foot route

¼ mile

WILTSHIRE

Wiltshire and Swindon Record Office,
Libraries & Heritage H.Q.,
Trowbridge BA14 8BS.
Tel: 01225 713138;
Fax: 01225 713515.
Email: wsro@wiltshire.gov.uk
Website: www.wiltshire.gov.uk

CARN ticket required.

TROWBRIDGE

¼ mile

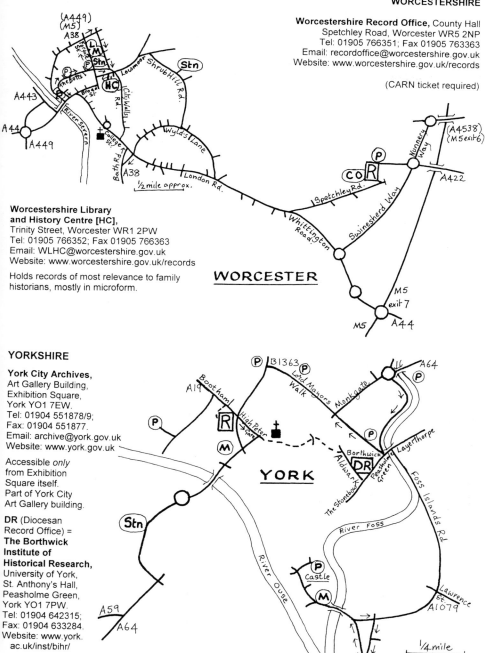

WORCESTERSHIRE

Worcestershire Record Office, County Hall
Spetchley Road, Worcester WR5 2NP
Tel: 01905 766351; Fax 01905 763363
Email: recordoffice@worcestershire.gov.uk
Website: www.worcestershire.gov.uk/records

(CARN ticket required)

**Worcestershire Library
and History Centre [HC],**
Trinity Street, Worcester WR1 2PW
Tel: 01905 766352; Fax 01905 766363
Email: WLHC@worcestershire.gov.uk
Website: www.worcestershire.gov.uk/records

Holds records of most relevance to family
historians, mostly in microform.

WORCESTER

YORKSHIRE

York City Archives,
Art Gallery Building,
Exhibition Square,
York YO1 7EW.
Tel: 01904 551878/9;
Fax: 01904 551877.
Email: archive@york.gov.uk
Website: www.york.gov.uk

Accessible *only*
from Exhibition
Square itself.
Part of York City
Art Gallery building.

DR (Diocesan
Record Office) =
**The Borthwick
Institute of
Historical Research,**
University of York,
St. Anthony's Hall,
Peasholme Green,
York YO1 7PW.
Tel: 01904 642315;
Fax: 01904 633284.
Website: www.york.
ac.uk/inst/bihr/

YORK

YORKSHIRE: EAST RIDING

East Riding of Yorkshire Archives Service,
County Hall,
Beverley HU17 9BA.
Tel: 01482 392790; Fax: 01482 392791.
Email: archives.service@eastriding.gov.uk
Website: www.eastriding.gov.uk/learning

The archives office is located at the chapel
in Lord Roberts Road.

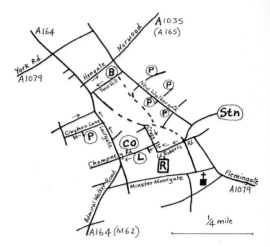

BEVERLEY

KINGSTON UPON HULL

Hull City Archives,
79 Lowgate, Hull HU1 1HN.
Tel: 01482 615102;
Fax: 01482 613051.
Email: City.archives@hullcc.gov.uk

YORKSHIRE: NORTH RIDING

North Yorkshire County Record Office,
Malpas Road,
Northallerton, North Yorkshire.
Tel: 01609 777585; Fax: 01609 777078.
Website: www.northyorks.gov.uk/libraries

All correspondence to
North Yorkshire Record Office,
County Hall, Northallerton,
North Yorkshire DL7 8AF.

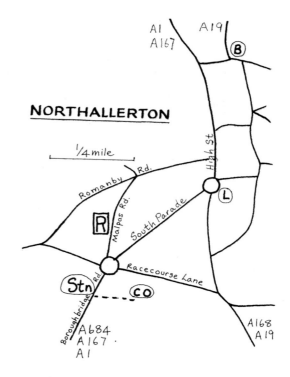

[R]···Record Office
CO···County Offices
L···Library
M···Museum
P···Car Park
B···Bus Station
Stn··Railway Station
----·Foot route

Teesside Archives,
Exchange House, 6 Marton Road,
Middlesbrough TS1 1DB.
Tel: 01642 248321; Fax 01642 248391.
Email: teesside_archives@middlesbrough.gov.uk

CARN ticket required.

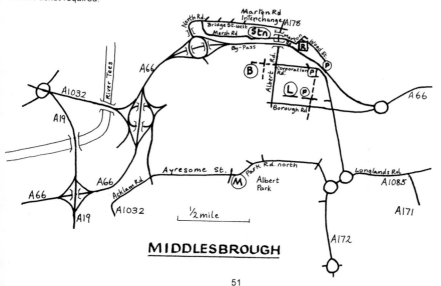

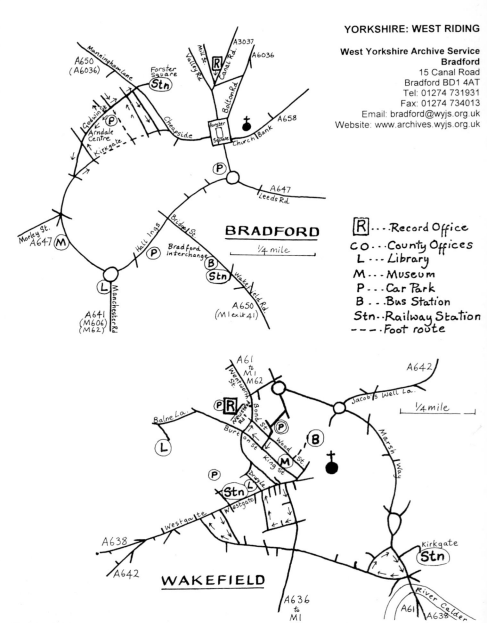

YORKSHIRE: WEST RIDING

West Yorkshire Archive Service
Bradford
15 Canal Road
Bradford BD1 4AT
Tel: 01274 731931
Fax: 01274 734013
Email: bradford@wyjs.org.uk
Website: www.archives.wyjs.org.uk

BRADFORD

¼ mile

R ···Record Office
CO···County Offices
L ···Library
M···Museum
P···Car Park
B··Bus Station
Stn··Railway Station
----·Foot route

WAKEFIELD

¼ mile

West Yorkshire Archive Service H.Q., Registry of Deeds,
Newstead Road, Wakefield WF1 2DE.
Tel: 01924 305980; Fax 01924 305983.
Email: wakefield@wyjs.org.uk
Website: www.archives.wyjs.org.uk/

YORKSHIRE: WEST RIDING

West Yorkshire Archive Service:
Calderdale,
Calderdale Central Library,
Northgate House, Northgate,
Halifax HX1 1UN.
Tel: 01422 392636;
Fax: 01422 341083.
Email: calderdale@wyjs.org.uk
Website: www.archives.wyjs.org.uk/

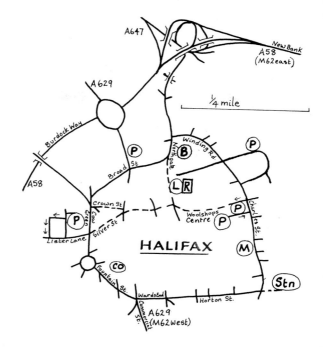

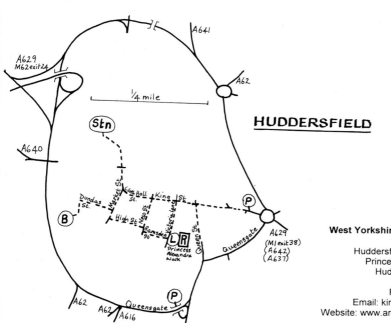

West Yorkshire Archive Service
Kirklees
Huddersfield Central Library
Princess Alexandra Walk
Huddersfield HD1 2SU
Tel: 01484 221966
Fax: 01484 518361
Email: kirklees@wyjs.org.uk
Website: www.archives.wyjs.org.uk/

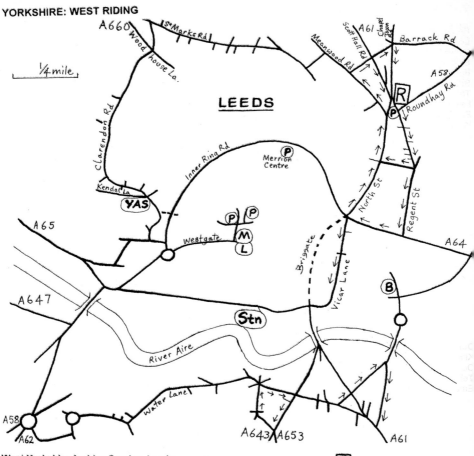

West Yorkshire Archive Service, Leeds
Chapeltown Road, Sheepscar,
Leeds LS7 3AP.
Tel: 0113 214 5814; Fax: 0113 214 5815.
Email: enq@wyashq.demon.co.uk
Website: www.archives.wyjs.org.uk/

Yorkshire Archaeological Society,
West Yorkshire Archive Service,
Claremont, 23 Clarendon Road,
Leeds LS2 9NZ.
Tel: 0113 245 6362; Fax: 0113 244 1979.
Email and web as Leeds District Archives.

R ··· Record Office
CO ··· County Offices
L ··· Library
M ··· Museum
P ··· Car Park
B ·· Bus Station
Stn·· Railway Station
– – – ·Foot route

YORKSHIRE: WEST RIDING

**Barnsley Archive and
Local Studies Department,**
Central Library,
Shambles Street,
Barnsley,
South Yorkshire S70 2JF.
Tel: 01226 773950;
Fax: 01226 773955.
Email: archives@barnsley.gov.uk
Website: www.barnsley.gov

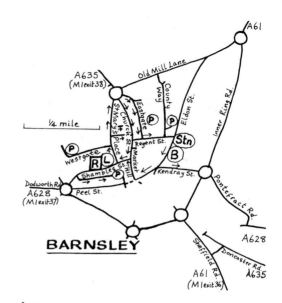

Doncaster Archives,
King Edward Road, Balby,
Doncaster DN4 0NA.
Tel: 01302 859811.
Email: doncaster.archives@doncaster.gov.uk

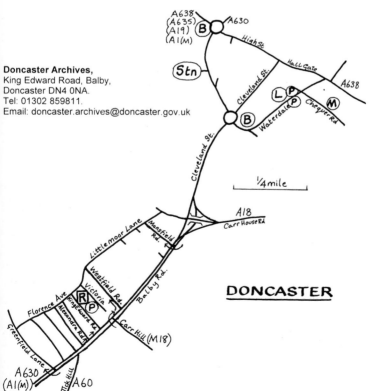

YORKSHIRE: WEST RIDING

Rotherham Metropolitan
Borough Archives and
Local Studies Section,
Central Library, Walker Place,
Rotherham S65 1JH.
Tel: 01709 823616;
Fax: 01709 823650.
Email: archives@rotherham.gov.uk
Website: www.rotherham.
   gov.uk/find/archives.htm

R ... Record Office
CO ... County Offices
L ... Library
M ... Museum
P ... Car Park
B ... Bus Station
Stn ... Railway Station
---- Foot route

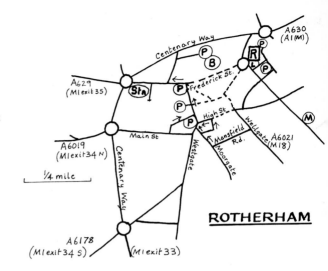

ROTHERHAM

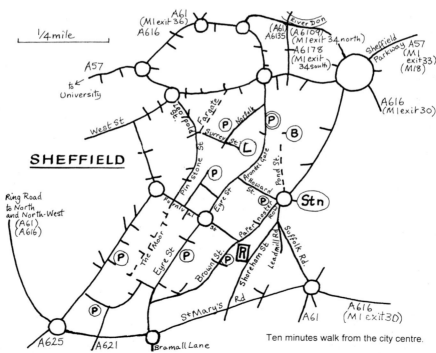

SHEFFIELD

Ten minutes walk from the city centre.

Sheffield Archives, 52 Shoreham Street, Sheffield S1 4SP. Tel: 0114 203 9395; Fax: 0114 203 9398.
Email: sheffield.archives@dial.pipex.com
Website: www:earl.org.uk/earl/members/sheffield/arch.htm

WALES

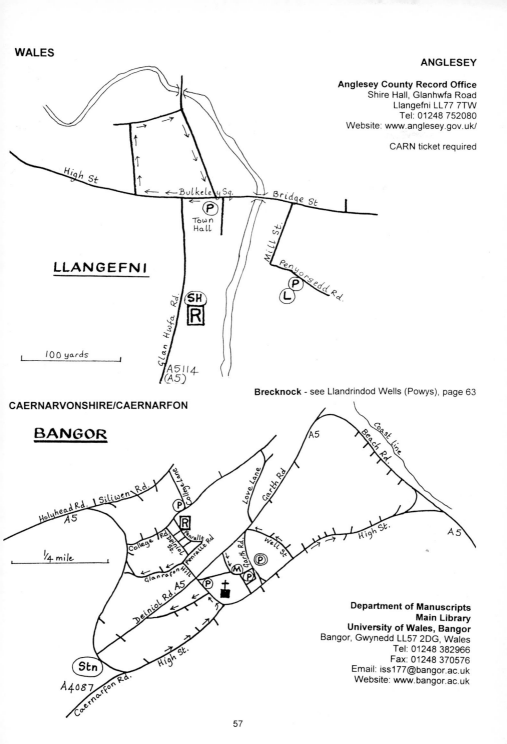

ANGLESEY

Anglesey County Record Office
Shire Hall, Glanhwfa Road
Llangefni LL77 7TW
Tel: 01248 752080
Website: www.anglesey.gov.uk/

CARN ticket required

LLANGEFNI

High St

← Bulkeley Sq.

Bridge St

Mill St.

Penyorsedd Rd.

Town Hall

Glan Hwfa Rd.

A5114
(A5)

100 yards

Brecknock - see Llandrindod Wells (Powys), page 63

CAERNARVONSHIRE/CAERNARFON

BANGOR

Holyhead Rd.
A5

Siliwen Rd.

College Rd.

Coast Line

Beach Rd.

A5

Love Lane

Garth Rd.

College Rd. Penrallt Rd.

Deiniol St.

Glanrafon Hill

Well St.

High St.

A5

Garth Rd.

¼ mile

Glanrafon A5

Deiniol Rd. A5

Caernarfon Rd.

High St.

Stn

A4087

Department of Manuscripts
Main Library
University of Wales, Bangor
Bangor, Gwynedd LL57 2DG, Wales
Tel: 01248 382966
Fax: 01248 370576
Email: iss177@bangor.ac.uk
Website: www.bangor.ac.uk

57

WALES: CAERNARVONSHIRE/CAERNARFON

Caernarfon Record Office,
Gwynedd Archives and Museums Service,
Victoria Dock, Caernarfon.
Tel: 01286 679095; Fax: 01286 679637.
Email: archives@gwynedd.gov.uk
Website: www.gwynedd.gov.uk/Archives

Correspondence to
Education and Culture Department,
County Offices, Shirehall Street,
Caernarfon LL55 1SH.

CARN ticket required.

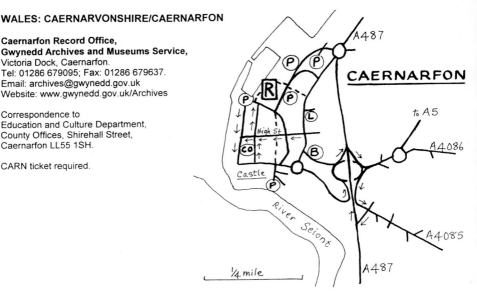

CAERNARFON

R....Record Office
CO...County Offices
L...Library
M...Museum
P...Car Park
B...Bus Station
Stn..Railway Station
----.Foot route

CARDIGANSHIRE/CEREDIGION

National Library of
Wales (N.L.W.),
Department of Manuscripts
and Records,
Penglais,
Aberystwyth SY23 3BU.
Tel: 01970 632800;
Fax: 01970 632883.
Email: holi@llgc.org.uk
Website: www.llgc.org.uk/

Ceredigion (Cardiganshire)
Archives/
Archifdy Ceredigion,
County Offices/Swydd'far Sir,
Marine Terrace/Glan-y-Mor,
Aberystwyth SY23 2DE.
Tel: 01970 633697/8;
Fax: 01970 633663.
Email:
archives@ceredigion.gov.uk.
Website:
www.llgc.org.uk/cac/
cac0009.htm

CARN ticket required.

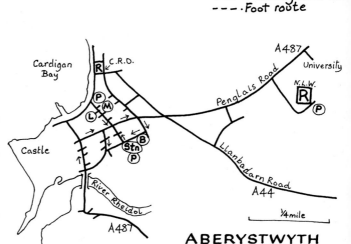

ABERYSTWYTH

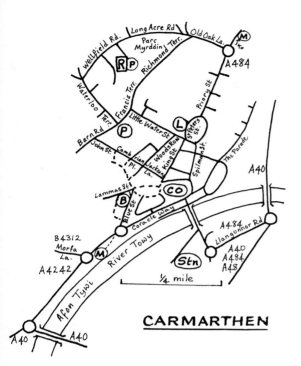

WALES: CARMARTHENSHIRE

Carmarthenshire Archives Service
Parc Myrddin, Richmond Terrace
Carmarthen SA31 1DS
Tel: 01267 228232; Fax: 01267 228237
Email: archives@carmarthenshire.gov.uk

CARMARTHEN

DENBIGHSHIRE

Denbighshire Record Office
46 Clwyd Street
Ruthin LL15 1HP
Tel: 01824 708250
Fax 01824 708258
Email: archives@
denbighshire.gov.uk
Website: www.
denbighshire.gov.uk/

CARN ticket required

RUTHIN

59

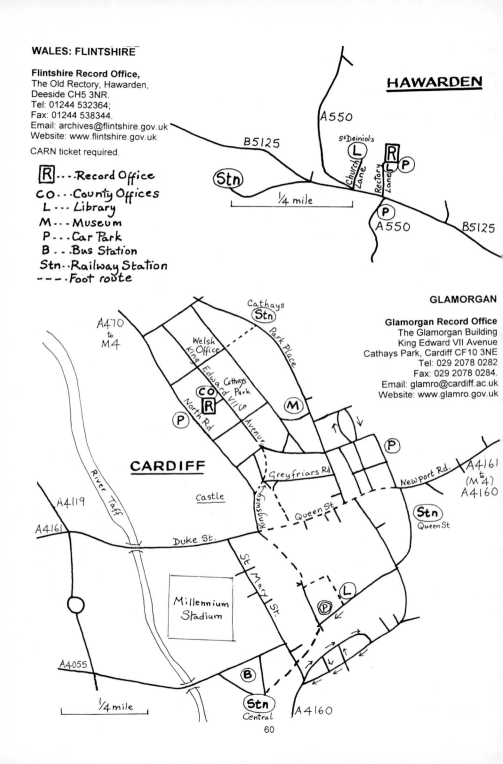

WALES: FLINTSHIRE

Flintshire Record Office,
The Old Rectory, Hawarden,
Deeside CH5 3NR.
Tel: 01244 532364;
Fax: 01244 538344.
Email: archives@flintshire.gov.uk
Website: www.flintshire.gov.uk

CARN ticket required.

R ... Record Office
CO ... County Offices
L ... Library
M ... Museum
P ... Car Park
B ... Bus Station
Stn .. Railway Station
- - - - Foot route

HAWARDEN

A550
B5125
St Deiniol's
Church Lane
Rectory Lane
¼ mile
A550
B5125
Stn

GLAMORGAN

Glamorgan Record Office
The Glamorgan Building
King Edward VII Avenue
Cathays Park, Cardiff CF10 3NE
Tel: 029 2078 0282
Fax: 029 2078 0284.
Email: glamro@cardiff.ac.uk
Website: www.glamro.gov.uk

CARDIFF

A470 to M4
Cathays Stn
Welsh Office
King Edward VII Avenue
Cathays Park
Park Place
North Rd
M
CO R
P
Greyfriars Rd
Kingsway
Castle
Queen St
Newport Rd.
A4161 (M4) to A4160
Stn Queen St
River Taff
A4119
A4161
Duke St.
St Mary St.
Millennium Stadium
P
L
A4055
B
Stn Central
A4160
¼ mile

WALES: GLAMORGAN

West Glamorgan Archive Service,
County Hall, Oystermouth Road,
Swansea SA1 3SN.
Tel: 01792 636589; Fax: 01792 637130.
Email: susan.beckley@swansea.gov.uk
Website: www.swansea.gov.uk/archives

SWANSEA

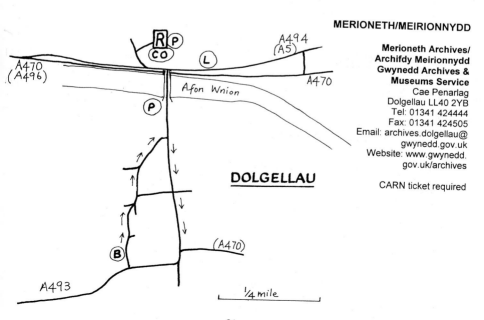

MERIONETH/MEIRIONNYDD

**Merioneth Archives/
Archifdy Meirionnydd
Gwynedd Archives &
Museums Service**
Cae Penarlag
Dolgellau LL40 2YB
Tel: 01341 424444
Fax: 01341 424505
Email: archives.dolgellau@
gwynedd.gov.uk
Website: www.gwynedd.
gov.uk/archives

CARN ticket required

DOLGELLAU

WALES

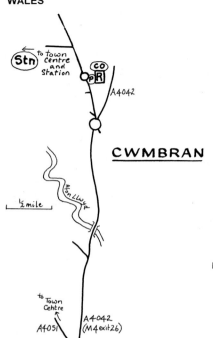

CWMBRAN

MONMOUTHSHIRE

Gwent Record Office
County Hall, Cwmbran
Gwent NP44 2XH
Tel: 01633 644886; Fax 01633 648382
Email: gwent.records@torfaen.gov.uk
Website: www.llgc.org.uk/cac/cac0004.htm

Bus service from Newport passes County Hall

CARN ticket required

Montgomeryshire – see Llandrindod.Wells (Powys), page 63.

R ...Record Office
CO...County Offices
L ...Library
M...Museum
P...Car Park
B ..Bus Station
Stn..Railway Station
----.Foot route

PEMBROKESHIRE

HAVERFORDWEST

Pembrokeshire Record Office,
The Castle,
Haverfordwest SA61 2EF.
Tel: 01437 763707.
Fax: 01437 768539
Email: Record.Office@
   pembrokeshire.gov.uk

WALES: POWYS
(Brecknock, Montgomryshire, Radnorshire)

Powys County Archives Office,
County Hall,
Llandrindod Wells,
Powys LD1 5LG.
Tel: 01597 826088;
Fax 01597 826087
Email: archives@powys.gov.uk
Website: www.archives.powys.gov.uk/

CARN ticket required.

ISLE OF MAN

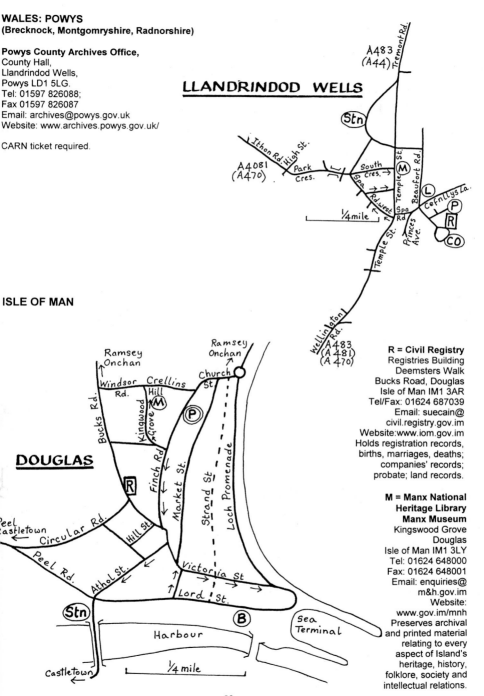

R = Civil Registry
Registries Building
Deemsters Walk
Bucks Road, Douglas
Isle of Man IM1 3AR
Tel/Fax: 01624 687039
Email: suecain@
civil.registry.gov.im
Website:www.iom.gov.im
Holds registration records,
births, marriages, deaths;
companies' records;
probate; land records.

**M = Manx National
Heritage Library
Manx Museum**
Kingswood Grove
Douglas
Isle of Man IM1 3LY
Tel: 01624 648000
Fax: 01624 648001
Email: enquiries@
m&h.gov.im
Website:
www.gov.im/mnh
Preserves archival
and printed material
relating to every
aspect of Island's
heritage, history,
folklore, society and
intellectual relations.

SCOTLAND

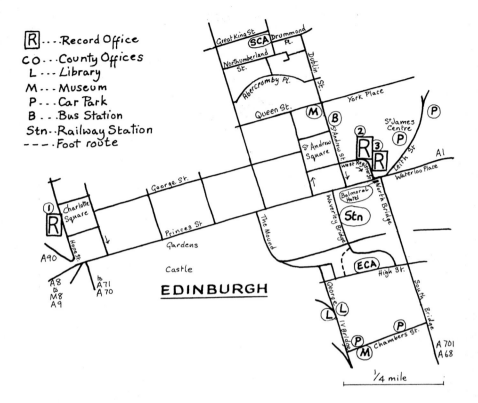

3: The National Archives of Scotland,
formerly the
Scottish Record Office,
H.M. General Register House,
Princes Street, Edinburgh EH1 3YY
Tel: 0131 535 1314; Fax: 0131 535 1360
Email: research@nas.gov.uk
Website: www.nas.gov.uk
and

1: West Register House,
Charlotte Square, Edinburgh EH2 4DF.

2: General Register Office for Scotland
(Birth/Marriage/Death Certificates; Census;
Parish Registers)
New Register House,
Edinburgh EH1 3YT.
Tel: 0131 334 0380; Fax: 0131 314 4400.
Email: gros@gtnet.gov.uk.co
Website: www.gro-scotland.gov.uk

Entrance in West Register Street,

L: National Library of Scotland,
Department of Manuscripts,
George IV Bridge, Edinburgh EH1 1EW.
Tel: 0131-226 4531; Fax: 0131 466 2804
Email: mss@nls.uk
Website: www.nls.uk/

ECA: Edinburgh City Archives,
Department of Corporate Services,
City of Edinburgh Council, City Chambers,
High Street, Edinburgh EH1 1YJ.
Tel: 0131 529 4616; Fax: 0131 529 4957.

Scottish Catholic Archives,
Columba House, 16 Drummond Place,
Edinburgh EH3 6PL.
Tel: 0131 556 3661.
(by appointment only).